TypeScript for DevOps

The Secret Weapon for Automating, Scaling, and Securing Your Infrastructure

Adriam Miller

2

3

Discover Other Books in the Series

"TypeScript for Beginners: A Beginner's Guide to the Future of JavaScript"

"TypeScript for Backend Development: Backend applications with Node.js, Express, and modern frameworks"

"TypeScript for Blockchain: Unlock the full potential of TypeScript in Web3 development"

"Typescript for Front End Development: Reduce Errors, Boost Productivity, and Master Modern Web Development Like a Pro"

"TypeScript for JavaScript Developers: The Essential Guide for JavaScript Developers to Write Safer, Scalable, and More Efficient Code"

"Typescript for Microservices: Learn How to Leverage TypeScript to Develop Robust, Maintainable, and Efficient Microservices Architecture"

"TypeScript for Mobile Application Development: Build Faster, Safer, and Smarter Applications with Ease"

"TypeScript for Web Development: Boost Your Productivity, Eliminate Costly Errors, and Build Scalable Web Applications with TypeScript"

Printed in the United States of America.

For more information, or to book an event, contact :
(Email & Website)

Book design by Adriam Miller
Cover design by Adriam Miller

Disclaimer

The information provided in *"TypeScript for DevOps: The Secret Weapon for Automating, Scaling, and Securing Your Infrastructure"* by Adrian Miller is for **educational and informational purposes only**.

This Book is designed to provide insights into TypeScript programming and its applications in blockchain and Web3 development.

Introduction

Welcome to "TypeScript for DevOps: The Secret Weapon for Automating, Scaling, and Securing Your Infrastructure." In an era characterized by rapid technological advancement, the challenges faced by developers and operations teams are becoming increasingly intricate. As the distinction between development and operations diminishes, adopting a comprehensive and effective strategy for infrastructure management is more essential than ever. This is where TypeScript plays a pivotal role—not merely as a programming language, but as a formidable asset that can enhance your DevOps methodologies.

TypeScript, which is a superset of JavaScript, brings static typing and sophisticated tooling to the realm of web development, allowing developers to produce code that is more predictable and easier to maintain. However, its advantages reach well beyond front-end development. When integrated into DevOps practices, TypeScript can facilitate automation, improve infrastructure as code (IaC) processes, and strengthen security protocols throughout your environment.

In this book, we will delve into how TypeScript can become the cornerstone of your DevOps framework. We will examine practical applications in automation using tools such as AWS CDK and Terraform, strategies for scaling to meet evolving demands, and the implementation of security best practices to safeguard your infrastructure against potential threats.

Whether you are an experienced DevOps expert, a developer seeking to broaden your skill set, or a newcomer

7

to the field, this book will offer valuable insights and practical guidance. You will learn how to leverage TypeScript to write clearer, error-resistant scripts that automate deployment processes, manage infrastructure with greater agility, and secure sensitive data with confidence. By the end of this journey, you will see TypeScript not just as a language, but as your secret weapon in the evolving landscape of DevOps.

Join us as we unlock the potential of TypeScript in transforming the way you approach automation, scaling, and security in your infrastructure. Let's harness the power of TypeScript together and take your DevOps practices to new heights!

Chapter 1: TypeScript Fundamentals for DevOps

For professionals in the DevOps field, acquiring knowledge of TypeScript is essential—not only for crafting robust and maintainable code but also for promoting effective collaboration between development and operations teams. This chapter provides an introduction to the fundamental concepts of TypeScript, with the goal of equipping you with the necessary insights for implementing DevOps practices.

What is TypeScript?

TypeScript is a superset of JavaScript created by Microsoft, aimed at simplifying the development of large-scale applications. It incorporates static typing, allowing developers to define types for variables, function parameters, and return values. This feature aids in identifying errors during the compilation process rather than at runtime, thereby enhancing code quality and maintainability.

Key Features of TypeScript

Static Typing: In contrast to JavaScript's dynamic typing, TypeScript enables explicit type definitions, which helps mitigate bugs by ensuring that values adhere to the expected types.

Interfaces: TypeScript introduces the concept of interfaces, allowing developers to establish contracts for objects. This promotes improved code organization and the creation of reusable components, which are valuable attributes in DevOps methodologies.

Classes and Inheritance: TypeScript upholds the principles of object-oriented programming through the use of classes, interfaces, and inheritance, facilitating the development of complex software systems that are more manageable and scalable.**Type Inference**: Even though TypeScript is statically typed, it supports type inference, allowing you to omit type annotations when the compiler can infer them automatically.

Enhanced Tooling: TypeScript's integration with modern IDEs like Visual Studio Code enhances the development experience through features like autocompletion, real-time error checking, and refactoring tools.

Setting Up TypeScript

Before diving into TypeScript, it's essential to set up an environment where you can write and execute your TypeScript code. Here's how you can get started:

Install Node.js: TypeScript runs on Node.js, so the first step is to ensure you have Node.js installed on your machine. Download it from the [Node.js official website](https://nodejs.org) and follow the installation instructions.

Install TypeScript: With Node.js installed, you can install TypeScript globally using npm (Node Package Manager) by running the following command in your terminal:

```bash
npm install -g typescript
```

Create a Project: Initialize a new TypeScript project by creating a new directory and navigating to it. Run the following command to create a basic TypeScript configuration file:

```bash
tsc --init
```

Write Your First TypeScript Code: Create a new file called `app.ts` and write your first TypeScript code:

```typescript
const greeting: string = "Hello, TypeScript!";
console.log(greeting);
```

Compile to JavaScript: TypeScript needs to be compiled into JavaScript before it can be executed in a JavaScript runtime. To compile, run the following command:

```bash
tsc app.ts
```

This will create a file called `app.js` that you can run using Node.js:

```bash
node app.js
```

Type System Basics

Understanding the type system is essential for harnessing TypeScript's power effectively. Here are the fundamental types you should familiarize yourself with:

Basic Types:

`string`: Represents textual data.

`number`: Represents numeric values, both integers and floating-point numbers.

`boolean`: Represents a true or false value.

`any`: A flexible type that can hold any value, useful for dynamic scenarios but should be used sparingly.

Arrays: TypeScript allows you to create arrays of specific types, which enhances type safety.

```typescript
let numbers: number[] = [1, 2, 3];
```

Tuples: Tuples are arrays with a fixed number of elements where each element can have a different type.

```typescript
let user: [string, number] = ['Alice', 25];
```

Enums: Enums are a way to define a set of named constants, making your code easier to read and maintain.

```typescript
enum Direction {
Up, Down, Left, Right
}
```

Function Types: Functions can have specified types

12

for their parameters and return values, enhancing clarity and preventing potential errors.

```typescript
function add(a: number, b: number): number { return a + b;
}
```

Advanced TypeScript Concepts

Once you grasp the basics, it's worth delving into some advanced features that can be especially beneficial in a DevOps context:

Generics

Generics enable you to write code that works with any data type while preserving type information. This is particularly useful in creating reusable code components.

```typescript
function identity<T>(arg: T): T { return arg;
}
```

Type Guards

Type guards are conditional blocks that ensure types are correctly inferred within specific scopes, allowing for more robust type checking.

```typescript
function printId(id: number | string) { if (typeof id === "string") {
```

```
console.log("String ID: " + id);
} else {
console.log("Number ID: " + id);
}
}
```
` ` `

Utility Types

TypeScript comes with several built-in utility types that help manipulate types easily:

`Partial<T>`: Constructs a type with all properties of T set to optional.

`Readonly<T>`: Constructs a type with all properties of T set to readonly.

`Pick<T, K>`: Constructs a type by picking the set of properties K from T.

By understanding TypeScript's type system, leveraging its advanced features, and integrating it into your DevOps pipeline, you can improve code quality, foster collaboration, and streamline the development lifecycle.

Understanding TypeScript: Key Concepts and Benefits

JavaScript, the de facto language of the web, provides the foundation for dynamic web applications. However, as projects scale and teams expand, developers often encounter the challenges of managing large codebases, tracking down bugs, and ensuring code quality. This is where TypeScript comes into play.

Created by Microsoft and first released in 2012, TypeScript is a superset of JavaScript that introduces static typing to the language. By allowing developers to specify types for variables, function parameters, and return values, TypeScript helps to catch errors early in the development process, making code more predictable and maintainable. This chapter explores the key concepts behind TypeScript and the benefits it offers to developers and teams, enabling them to write better code and improve their overall development workflow.

Key Concepts of TypeScript ### 1. Static Typing

At its core, TypeScript introduces static typing to JavaScript. This means that developers can specify data types such as `string`, `number`, `boolean`, `array`, and custom types. Static typing allows for early detection of type-related errors through compile-time checks rather than runtime errors, which can significantly reduce debugging efforts.

For example, consider the following function written in JavaScript:

```javascript
function add(a, b) {

return a + b;

}
```

In JavaScript, the types of `a` and `b` are dynamic and can lead to unexpected results:

15

```javascript
console.log(add(5, 10));    // 15
console.log(add("5", "10"));        // "510"
```

In TypeScript, you can specify that `a` and `b` should be numbers:

```typescript
function add(a: number, b: number): number { return a +
b;
}
```

Now, if you try to pass strings to this function, TypeScript will raise an error during compilation:

```typescript
console.log(add(5, 10));    // 15

console.log(add("5", "10"));        // Error: Argument of
type 'string' is not assignable to parameter of type
'number'.
```

2. Interfaces and Type Aliases

TypeScript allows developers to define custom shapes for their data through interfaces and type aliases. This provides a way to enforce object structures, making the code more readable and maintainable.

An interface defines a structure that an object can conform to:

16

```typescript
interface User {
  id: number; name: string; isActive: boolean;
}
const user: User = { id: 1,
name: "Alice", isActive: true
};
```

Type aliases can be used for more complex types or unions:

```typescript
type Point = {
x: number; y: number;
};
type ID = string | number;
```

3. Union and Intersection Types

TypeScript supports union and intersection types, which enable developers to create more expressive type definitions. A union type allows a value to be one of several types, while an intersection type combines multiple types into one.

For example:

```typescript
function logValue(value: string | number) {
console.log(value);
}
```

```
```

In this case, `logValue` can accept either a string or a number. With intersection types, you can combine multiple interfaces:

```typescript
interface Address {
street: string; city: string;
}
interface User { id: number; name: string;
}
type UserProfile = User & Address; const profile: UserProfile = {
id: 1,
name: "Alice",
street: "123 Main St", city: "Wonderland"
};
```

4. Generics

Generics provide a way to create reusable components in TypeScript. By allowing types to be passed as parameters, generics enable the creation of functions, classes, or interfaces that work with any data type.

For example, a generic function for a simple identity can be written as follows:

```typescript
```

```
function identity<T>(arg: T): T { return arg;

}

let output = identity<string>("Hello, TypeScript!"); let
outputNumber = identity<number>(42);

```
```

5. Rich Tooling and IDE Support

One of the most significant advantages of using TypeScript
is the rich tooling and integrated development
environment (IDE) support it offers. Popular editors like
Visual Studio Code provide features like IntelliSense,
autocompletion, type checking, and inline
documentation—all powered by TypeScript's type system.
This enhances developer productivity and reduces the
friction found in refactoring and navigating large
codebases.

Benefits of Using TypeScript ### 1. Improved Code
Quality

By catching type-related errors at compile time,
TypeScript helps improve code quality significantly.
Developers can identify and fix issues before they reach
production, reducing the number of bugs and making it
easier to maintain code.

2. Enhanced Collaboration

TypeScript's explicit type definitions provide clear
documentation for code, making it easier for team
members to understand the intended use of functions and
objects. This promotes better collaboration within
development teams, especially in larger projects where
multiple developers need to work on the same codebase.
```

3. Scalability

TypeScript is designed for large-scale applications. Its features, such as modules, interfaces, and namespaces, allow developers to organize code more effectively. This modularity and clear structure contribute to easier scaling of applications over time.

4. Compatibility with JavaScript

TypeScript is fully compatible with existing JavaScript code. Developers can gradually adopt TypeScript in their projects by renaming `.js` files to `.ts` and adding type annotations as needed. This makes it easy to transition to TypeScript without a complete rewrite of existing code.

5. Future-Proofing

TypeScript provides access to upcoming JavaScript features through its implementation of ECMAScript proposals. This allows developers to use modern JavaScript features while maintaining compatibility with older environments.

TypeScript is more than just a language; it's a powerful tool that enhances the development experience. By introducing static typing and other advanced features, TypeScript helps developers create more robust, maintainable, and scalable applications.

Setting Up a TypeScript Development Environment for DevOps

One of the essential elements of this approach is establishing efficient and effective development environments. When working with TypeScript, a powerful, statically typed superset of JavaScript, creating a well-configured setup can enhance productivity, ensure code quality, and streamline deployment processes. This chapter will guide you through setting up a TypeScript development environment tailored for DevOps workflows.

1. Prerequisites

Before diving into the setup process, ensure that you have the following prerequisites:

Node.js: TypeScript relies on Node.js for package management and execution. Download and install the latest version from the [official Node.js website](https://nodejs.org/).

TypeScript: Once Node.js is installed, you can install TypeScript globally using npm (Node Package Manager). Open your terminal and run:

```bash
npm install -g typescript
```

Package Manager: Familiarize yourself with npm or yarn, as they will be instrumental in managing your project's dependencies.

2. Initializing a TypeScript Project

To begin, create a directory for your TypeScript project and initialize it:

```bash
mkdir my-typescript-project cd my-typescript-project npm init -y
```

21

```
```

This command creates a `package.json` file, which is essential for managing your project's dependencies and scripts.

3. Installing TypeScript Locally

While you can run TypeScript globally, it's good practice to install it locally within each project for consistency. To install TypeScript as a development dependency, run:

```bash
npm install typescript --save-dev
```

Following this, you can set up a `tsconfig.json` file, which configures the TypeScript compiler options. To generate a default configuration, execute:

```bash
npx tsc --init
```

This command creates a `tsconfig.json` file with default settings. You can customize it based on your project requirements.

4. Setting Up Node.js Development Environment ### 4.1. Editor Configuration

Choose a code editor that supports TypeScript and provides extensions for better development experience. Popular options include:

Visual Studio Code: A widely-used IDE with excellent TypeScript support and a rich ecosystem of extensions. For development, consider installing:

Prettier: For code formatting.

ESLint: For linting TypeScript code.

TypeScript Hero: For managing imports. #### Sample VSCode Configuration

To enhance your development experience, you can create a `.vscode` directory in your project with the following recommended settings (`settings.json`):

```json
{
"editor.formatOnSave":                                  true,
"editor.codeActionsOnSave": { "source.fixAll eslint": true
},
"typescript.suggest.autoImports":                       true,
"typescript.tsserver.trace": "messages"
}
```

4.2. TypeScript Compiler Options

In the `tsconfig.json` file, configure the compiler options according to the type of application you are developing. Here's an example configuration for a Node.js application:

```json
{
"compilerOptions":   {   "target":   "ES6",   "module":
```

```
"commonjs", "strict": true, "esModuleInterop": true,
"forceConsistentCasingInFileNames": true, "outDir":
"./dist",
"rootDir": "./src", "skipLibCheck": true
},
"include": ["src/**/*"],


"exclude": ["node_modules", "**/*.spec.ts"]
}
```

5. Integrating DevOps Tools

To align your TypeScript development environment with DevOps practices, consider integrating the following tools:

5.1. Version Control: Git

Git should already be familiar to most developers. Initialize a Git repository in your project:

```bash
git init
```

Then add a `.gitignore` file to exclude unnecessary files:

```
node_modules/ dist/
*.js
*.map
```

5.2. Continuous Integration (CI)

24

Set up CI tools like GitHub Actions, CircleCI, or Travis CI to automate testing and deployment. Here's a simple example using GitHub Actions:

Create a file in the `.github/workflows` directory called `ci.yml`:

```yaml
name: CI
```

on: [push, pull_request] jobs:

build:

runs-on: ubuntu-latest

steps:

name: Checkout code uses: actions/checkout@v2

name: Set up Node.js

uses: actions/setup-node@v2 with:

node-version: '16'

name: Install dependencies run: npm install

name: Compile TypeScript run: npm run build

name: Run tests run: npm test

This file ensures that every push or pull request triggers the CI process, checking out code, installing dependencies, building the application, and running tests.

5.3. Continuous Deployment (CD)

For continuous deployment, tools such as Docker can be invaluable. Create a `Dockerfile` to containerize your application:

```dockerfile
FROM node:16
```

WORKDIR /usr/src/app

COPY package*.json ./ RUN npm install COPY ./dist ./dist
CMD ["node", "dist/index.js"]
```

Build your Docker image and run the container:
```bash

docker build -t my-typescript-app .

docker run -p 3000:3000 my-typescript-app
```

6. Testing and Quality Assurance

To ensure your TypeScript code stands the test of time and meets high-quality standards, integrate testing frameworks and tools. Popular options include:

Jest: For unit testing.

Supertest: For testing HTTP endpoints. Install Jest and its TypeScript support:
```bash

npm install --save-dev jest ts-jest @types/jest
```

Add a script in `package.json` for testing:
```json "scripts": {

"test": "jest"

}
```
```

By using the right tools, maintaining good practices, and maintaining a focus on collaboration, teams can ensure a smooth, efficient development process that enhances productivity and delivers high-quality software. With this chapter, you've learned the critical steps to set up your environment and integrate DevOps principles effectively.

Chapter 2: Writing Efficient and Scalable TypeScript Code

TypeScript, an increasingly popular superset of JavaScript, offers developers tools and features that enhance the development process. However, writing efficient and scalable TypeScript code requires a solid understanding of both TypeScript itself and the principles of software design. In this chapter, we will explore some best practices and techniques to help you write efficient, maintainable, and scalable TypeScript code.

2.1 Understanding TypeScript Basics

Before diving into best practices, it's essential to understand the core concepts of TypeScript. TypeScript adds optional static types to JavaScript, enabling developers to catch errors early in the development process. Familiarize yourself with basic TypeScript features such as:

Types: Primitive types (string, number, boolean), arrays, tuples, enums, and more.

Interfaces and Types: Defining contracts for objects that help you enforce type safety.

Generics: Creating reusable code components that work with a variety of types.

Modules: Organizing code into logical units for better maintainability.

Mastering these fundamentals is a crucial first step towards writing efficient TypeScript code. ## 2.2 Structuring Your Codebase

A well-structured codebase is vital for scalability and maintainability. Here are some guidelines for structuring your TypeScript projects:

Organize by Feature: Instead of separating files by type (e.g., components, services, models), consider organizing them by feature. This way, all related files (components, services, models) are co-located, making it easier to navigate the codebase.

Use Modules Wisely: Take advantage of TypeScript's module system to encapsulate functionality. Each module should have a single responsibility and expose only what is necessary. This approach enhances code reusability and prevents tight coupling.

Adopt a Naming Convention: Consistent naming conventions improve code readability. Use descriptive names for files, functions, and variables, making the purpose of each clear.

Maintain a Flat Directory Structure: Especially for larger projects, maintaining a flat structure can reduce complexity. Avoid deeply nested directories; instead, group files into folders logically, such as by feature or domain.

2.3 Leveraging Type Safety

Type safety is one of TypeScript's most powerful features. By defining clear types, you can reduce runtime errors and increase code robustness.

Use Interfaces for Complex Types: Whenever you define a complex object, use an interface or type alias. This approach not only enforces structure but also serves as documentation for the expected shape of the data.

Avoid Any: While `any` is available to bypass type checking, its overuse can lead to code that's as error-prone as vanilla JavaScript. Instead, strive to define appropriate types. Use `unknown` if you need to defer type checking.

Type Guards: Implement type guards to narrow down types at runtime. This approach is particularly beneficial when working with unions or handling data from external sources, thus ensuring the integrity of your types.

2.4 Writing Clean and Maintainable Code

Readable and maintainable code is essential, especially in large projects where multiple developers may work on the same codebase.

Leverage TypeScript Features: Use features such as optional chaining, nullish coalescing, and rest/spread operators to write concise and clear code. For instance, optional chaining (`?.`) allows safe access to deeply nested properties.

Avoid Magic Numbers and Strings: Replace magic values with constants or enums. This practice improves code clarity and makes it easier to change values in one place if necessary.

Utilize Comments Judiciously: While code should be self-documenting, comments can be beneficial to explain why certain decisions were made or to clarify complex logic. However, avoid redundancy; comments should supplement the code, not substitute for clarity.

2.5 Performance Optimization Techniques

Efficiency is just as important as maintainability when it comes to TypeScript code. Here are some optimization techniques:

Use Asynchronous Patterns: TypeScript's async/await syntax simplifies asynchronous code. Use Promises or Observables (from libraries like RxJS) wisely to handle asynchronous operations.

Avoid Unnecessary Computations: Memoize functions to cache results and avoid recalculating when inputs haven't changed. Libraries such as `lodash` provide utilities for this purpose.

Leverage Code Splitting: For large applications, split your code into smaller chunks using dynamic imports. This technique can significantly improve initial load times and performance.

2.6 Testing Your TypeScript Code

Testing is crucial for ensuring your code performs as expected and remains reliable as your codebase evolves.

Type-Driven Test Cases: Leverage TypeScript's type system when writing tests. Create test cases that use the defined types and interfaces to ensure that edge cases and type constraints are thoroughly tested.

Use a Testing Framework: Popular frameworks such as Jest or Mocha work well with TypeScript. Use these frameworks to write unit tests and ensure each module functions correctly.

Combine with Visual Regression Testing: For applications with substantial UI components, consider adding visual regression testing tools to ensure that your components render correctly without unintended changes.

By adopting a well-structured approach, leveraging type safety, and focusing on performance optimization, you'll be better prepared to tackle complex projects. As you

31

continue your TypeScript journey, always be mindful of how your code can evolve, ensuring it remains maintainable and efficient as your application grows.

Best Practices for Clean, Maintainable Code in DevOps Scripts

TypeScript has emerged as a popular language for scripting due to its static typing, scalability, and enhanced tooling support. However, the effectiveness of a TypeScript DevOps script relies not only on the choice of language but also on how well the code is structured and maintained. This chapter will explore best practices for writing clean, maintainable code in TypeScript, specifically targeted at DevOps scripts.

1. Consistent Code Style ### 1.1 Use a Style Guide

Adopting a style guide is crucial for maintaining consistency throughout your codebase. Standard guidelines such as the [Airbnb JavaScript Style Guide](https://github.com/airbnb/javascript) or the [TypeScript Deep Dive Style Guide](https://basarat.gitbook.io/typescript/) can serve as a solid foundation. Using a linter like ESLint with TypeScript support can help enforce these rules automatically.

1.2 Formatting Tools

Incorporating formatting tools like Prettier ensures that your code is not just syntactically correct but also visually consistent. Regularly formatting code before commits helps prevent style-related discussions during code reviews.

2. Modularity and Reusability ### 2.1 Break Down Large Scripts

Large scripts can become difficult to manage and understand. Breaking your code into smaller, reusable modules can significantly enhance readability. Each module should focus on a single responsibility— commonly referred to as the Single Responsibility Principle (SRP).

2.2 Use Functions and Classes

Encapsulate functionality within functions or classes. This helps to group related code, making it easier to understand and reuse. Ensure that functions are concise and perform a single task.

Example:

```typescript
class Deployment { constructor(private service: string) {}

public deploy(version: string): void { this.build(version); this.pushToRegistry(); this.restartService();
}

private build(version: string): void {
// Code to build the service


}
private pushToRegistry(): void {
// Code to push the built service to a container registry
}
```

```
private restartService(): void {

// Code to restart the service

}

}
```
\ \ \

3. Effective Error Handling ### 3.1 Use Try/Catch Smartly

In a DevOps context, many operations can fail (like API calls or deployments). Utilizing try/catch blocks can help you gracefully handle errors, allowing you to log useful information and possibly recover from failure.

3.2 Centralized Error Handling

Consider implementing a centralized logging and error handling strategy. This could involve creating an error handling function or utilizing libraries like `winston` for logging errors in a consistent manner across your scripts.

Example:

```typescript
async function executeDeployment(deployment: Deployment) { try {

await deployment.deploy('1.0.0');

} catch (error) { console.error('Deployment failed:', error);

// Additional logging or alerting mechanisms can be invoked here

}

}
```

```
```

4. Documentation

4.1 Comment with Purpose

While code should strive to be self-documenting, comments can clarify complex logic or document the purpose of functions. Avoid redundant comments and instead focus on explaining the "why" rather than the "what."

4.2 Use JSDoc

Using JSDoc can help generate documentation directly from the code. This is particularly useful for larger teams or public repositories.

Example:

```typescript
/**

Deploys the service to the cloud.

@param version The version of the service to deploy.

*/

public deploy(version: string): void {

// Logic for deployment

}
```

5. Leverage TypeScript Features ### 5.1 Type Annotations

One of TypeScript's primary benefits is static typing. Always use type annotations to clarify variable and function types. This reduces development errors and enhances code readability.

5.2 Interfaces and Types

Utilize interfaces and type aliases to define data structures and function contracts. This makes your code more predictable and easier to refactor.

Example:

```typescript
interface ServiceConfig { name: string;

version: string;

environment: 'development' | 'staging' | 'production';

}

function deployService(config: ServiceConfig): void {

// Deployment logic

}
```

6. Version Control

6.1 Commit Messages

Use meaningful commit messages that describe the reasoning behind changes. This aids in tracking the evolution of your scripts.

6.2 Branch Strategy

Implement a branching strategy (such as Git Flow or trunk-based development) to manage development, testing, and production deployments effectively. Consistently merging code in a timely manner helps minimize conflicts.

Writing clean and maintainable code in TypeScript for DevOps scripts is a multifaceted task requiring attention to detail and adherence to best practices. By focusing on consistent code style, modularity, effective error handling, thorough documentation, leveraging TypeScript features, and maintaining a rigorous version control process, developers can create scripts that are not only functional but also robust and easy to maintain.

Using TypeScript's Type System to Prevent Errors in Automation

Fortunately, TypeScript, with its rich type system, offers powerful tools that can help developers prevent errors right at the compile stage — long before the code runs. This chapter explores how TypeScript's type system can be effectively utilized to enhance automation scripts, ensuring greater reliability and maintainability.

1. Understanding TypeScript's Type System

TypeScript is a superset of JavaScript that introduces static typing to the language. In TypeScript, types are not just annotations; they are a fundamental part of the language that can provide insights into the structure of the data, enforce contracts in your code, and catch potential errors early in the development process. Key features of TypeScript's type system include:

Basic types: including `string`, `number`, `boolean`, `null`, `undefined`, `void`, and arrays.

Type inference: TypeScript can automatically infer

types based on context, reducing the need for explicit type declarations.

Union types: allowing variables to hold more than one type.

Intersection types: enabling the combination of multiple types into one.

Interfaces and type aliases: which help define custom types and enforce structure.

Generics: making it possible to create reusable components that work with a variety of types.

Through the effective use of these features, developers can build automation scripts that are less prone to errors and easier to understand.

2. Typing Functionality in Automation Scripts

One of the most common pitfalls in automation scripting comes from interacting with external APIs or services. With TypeScript, developers can define clear and strict interfaces that describe the expected shapes of data received from these interactions. By defining types for incoming data, we mitigate the risk of bugs arising from unexpected or malformed input. Here's an example:

```typescript
interface ApiResponse { id: number;

name: string; completed: boolean;

}

async function fetchTask(taskId: number): Promise<ApiResponse> { const response = await fetch(`https://api.example.com/tasks/${taskId}`); return
```

```
response.json();

}

async function processTask(taskId: number) { const task =
await fetchTask(taskId);

console.log(`Task ${task.name} is ${task.completed ?
'completed' : 'not completed'}.`);

}
```

By defining the `ApiResponse` interface, we ensure that
any JSON response we process conforms to the expected
shape. The TypeScript compiler will raise errors if we try
to access properties that don't exist on the type, helping us
catch potential issues early.

3. Preventing Common Errors with Type Guards

Type guards in TypeScript can help us refine our types,
providing additional safety against common runtime
errors. For instance, when dealing with union types, a
type guard can allow the TypeScript compiler to infer the
correct type.

Consider an automation scenario where we process
different types of tasks:

```typescript
type Task = { id: number; type: 'email'; recipient: string } |
{ id: number; type: 'report'; filePath: string };

function sendNotification(task: Task) { if (task.type ===
'email') {

console.log(`Sending email to ${task.recipient}`);
```

```
} else if (task.type === 'report') { console.log(`Generating
report from ${task.filePath}`);
  }
}
```
` ` `

In this case, the conditional checks ensure that we access
properties relevant to the specific task type, preventing
unnecessary runtime errors and ensuring that our logic
behaves as expected.

4. Leveraging Enums for Better Readability and Safety

When scripting automation tasks, using enumerations
(enums) can increase clarity and safety. Enums allow us to
define a set of named constant values, which can
represent the different states or types of tasks:

```typescript
```typescript enum TaskType { Email = 'email', Report =
'report',
}
interface EmailTask { id: number;
type: TaskType.Email; recipient: string;
}
interface ReportTask { id: number;
type: TaskType.Report; filePath: string;
}
type Task = EmailTask | ReportTask;

// Usage
```
```

```
function executeTask(task: Task) { switch (task.type) {
case TaskType.Email:
console.log(`Sending email to ${task.recipient}`); break;
case TaskType.Report:
console.log(`Generating report from ${task.filePath}`);
break;
}
}
```
```

Using enums enhances code readability by providing semantic meaning to task types. Additionally, if new task types are introduced, we only need to update our enum, making maintenance much simpler.

As automation scripts scale in complexity and size, leveraging TypeScript's type system is an effective strategy for minimizing errors and enhancing code maintainability. By embracing strong typing, defining clear interfaces, using type guards, and employing enums, developers can catch potential issues at compile time instead of runtime, resulting in cleaner, safer, and more reliable automation scripts.
```

Chapter 3: Automating Repetitive DevOps Tasks with TypeScript

DevOps practices aim to enhance collaboration between development and operations teams, improve software delivery speed, and reduce the manual work that often consumes precious time and resources. In this chapter, we explore how TypeScript can be leveraged to automate repetitive DevOps tasks, streamline workflows, and enhance team productivity.

3.1 Understanding the Role of DevOps Automation

Before diving into automation with TypeScript, it's important to recognize the types of tasks that are ripe for automation within the DevOps lifecycle. These tasks typically include:

Infrastructure Provisioning and Configuration Management: Automating the setup and management of environments using tools like Terraform, Ansible, or CloudFormation.

Continuous Integration and Continuous Deployment (CI/CD): Automating the testing and deployment process to ensure rapid, error-free releases.

Monitoring and Logging: Streamlining the processes for gathering, analyzing, and alerting on system metrics and logs.

Backup and Recovery: Automation of data backup processes and disaster recovery plans to ensure data integrity and availability.

Identifying repetitive tasks in these categories is the first step towards developing efficient automation scripts.

3.2 Setting Up Your TypeScript Environment

To begin automating your DevOps tasks with TypeScript, you first need to set up a suitable development environment. This includes:

Node.js: Install Node.js, which allows you to run JavaScript and TypeScript on the server side.

TypeScript Compiler: Install TypeScript globally using npm:

```bash
npm install -g typescript
```

Text Editor or IDE: Use any text editor that supports TypeScript. Popular options include Visual Studio Code, Atom, or WebStorm.

Project Initialization: Create a new project directory and initialize it with npm:

```bash
mkdir devops-automation cd devops-automation npm init -y
```

Installing Necessary Packages: Depending on the tasks you wish to automate, you may need additional npm packages. For example, if you're interfacing with cloud services, you might want to install the AWS SDK:

```bash
npm install aws-sdk
```

Creating tsconfig.json: Set up TypeScript configuration by creating a `tsconfig.json` file:

```json
{
"compilerOptions": { "target": "ES6", "module": "commonjs", "outDir": "./dist", "strict": true
},
"include": ["src/**/*"], "exclude": ["node_modules"]
}
```

3.3 Writing Your First Automation Script

Let's automate a simple task: creating a backup of a directory. This example will involve using the file system module and some basic logic to handle backups.

Step 1: Setting Up Your Script

Create a new directory named `src` in your project folder and inside, create a file called `backup.ts`. Here's a sample implementation:

```typescript
import fs from 'fs';

import path from 'path';

const sourceDir = path.join(__dirname, 'source'); const backupDir = path.join(__dirname, 'backup');
```

```
const backupFiles = () => {
if (!fs.existsSync(backupDir)) { fs.mkdirSync(backupDir);
}
fs.readdir(sourceDir, (err, files) => { if (err) {
console.error('Error reading source directory:', err);
return;
}
files.forEach(file => {
const sourceFile = path.join(sourceDir, file); const
backupFile = path.join(backupDir, file);
fs.copyFile(sourceFile, backupFile, err => { if (err) {
console.error(`Failed to back up ${file}: `, err);

} else {
console.log(`${file} backed up successfully.`);
}
});
});
});
};
backupFiles();
```
```

### Step 2: Running the Script

To execute your script, compile it using the TypeScript
```

compiler and run the output JavaScript file:

```bash
tsc
node dist/backup.js
```

You should see confirmation messages for each file being backed up. ## 3.4 Integrating TypeScript with CI/CD Systems

One of the powerful capabilities of TypeScript is its easy integration with CI/CD systems. Most CI/CD tools like Jenkins, GitLab CI/CD, and GitHub Actions allow you to define pipeline jobs using scripts, and those can be written in TypeScript to facilitate automating testing and deployment.

For example, integrating tests into a GitHub Actions workflow can be as simple as adding a TypeScript- based testing script:

```yaml
name: CI

on: [push, pull_request] jobs:

build:

runs-on: ubuntu-latest steps:

name: Check out code uses: actions/checkout@v2

name: Set up Node.js

uses: actions/setup-node@v2 with:

node-version: '14'

name: Install dependencies run: npm install

name: Run tests run: npm run test
```

```

```

3.5 Best Practices for TypeScript Automation Scripts

When writing TypeScript scripts to automate DevOps tasks, consider the following best practices:

Modular Structure: Organize your code into modules to enhance readability and maintainability.

Error Handling: Implement robust error handling to ensure that your scripts fail gracefully and provide useful feedback.

Logging: Integrate logging to keep track of script execution and errors. Third-party libraries like

`winston` can help with this.

Testing: Implement tests for your automation scripts to ensure they function as intended. Use frameworks like Jest or Mocha for testing.

Commenting and Documentation: Comment your code adequately and maintain documentation for your automation processes to facilitate team collaboration.

By harnessing the power of TypeScript, teams can write more maintainable, scalable, and type-safe scripts that ease the burden of manual work. As automation continues to be a key component of successful DevOps practices, familiarity with tools like TypeScript is an essential skill in the modern development landscape.

Building CLI Tools with TypeScript for DevOps Automation

This chapter will guide you through the process of building a simple but effective CLI tool using TypeScript, focusing on its application in DevOps automation.

Why TypeScript?

TypeScript is a superset of JavaScript that introduces static typing. This feature can significantly enhance code quality, reduce bugs, and improve maintainability—all of which are crucial for DevOps teams managing complex systems. Additionally, TypeScript's compatibility with Node.js makes it an ideal choice for developing CLI applications.

Setting Up Your Development Environment

Before diving into coding, let's set up our development environment.

Node.js Installation

Ensure you have Node.js installed. You can download it from nodejs.org.

Initialize Your Project

Create a new directory for your CLI tool and navigate into it:

```bash
mkdir my-cli-tool cd my-cli-tool
```

Initialize a new Node.js project:

```bash npm init -y
```

```
```

Install TypeScript

Install TypeScript and types for Node.js:

```bash
npm install typescript @types/node --save-dev
```

Create Configuration File

Create a `tsconfig.json` file to configure TypeScript:

```json
{
"compilerOptions": { "target": "ES6", "module": "commonjs", "outDir": "./dist",
"rootDir": "./src", "strict": true
},
"include": ["src/**/*"], "exclude": ["node_modules"]
}
```

Create Your Directory Structure Create the necessary directories and files:

```bash
bash mkdir src
touch src/index.ts
```

Writing Your First CLI Tool

Now that your environment is set up, let's create a simple

CLI tool that automates a commonly encountered DevOps task: checking the status of a web server.

Implementing the CLI Logic

Open the `src/index.ts` file and add the following code:

```typescript
import * as https from 'https';

const checkWebsiteStatus = (url: string) => {
https.get(url, (res) => {

const { statusCode } = res;

if (statusCode) {

console.log(`Website ${url} is up with status code: ${statusCode}`);

}

}).on('error', (e) => {

console.error(`Failed to reach ${url}: ${e.message}`);

});

};

const args = process.argv.slice(2); if (args.length === 0) {

console.error('Please provide a URL to check.');
process.exit(1);

}

const url = args[0]; checkWebsiteStatus(url);
```

Explanation of the Code

Importing Modules: We import the `https` module to make HTTP requests.

Function Definition: The `checkWebsiteStatus` function takes a URL, sends a GET request, and logs the status code.

Argument Handling: We can extract command-line arguments using `process.argv`, and we check if the user has provided a URL.

Execution: The script checks the status of the given URL and logs either the status code or an error message.

Compiling and Running the CLI Tool To compile your TypeScript code, run:

```bash
npx tsc
```

This will generate the compiled JavaScript files in the `dist` directory. You can now run the CLI tool using Node.js:

```bash
node dist/index.js https://www.example.com
```

If the server is up, you should see a message like:

```
Website https://www.example.com is up with status code: 200
```

Enhancing Your CLI Tool

While the above implementation serves a fundamental purpose, modern CLI applications often require additional features:

1. Command-Line Argument Parsing

For more complex command-line interfaces, libraries such as `yargs` or `commander` can make argument parsing easier.

To install `yargs`, use:

```bash
npm install yargs
```

Update your `src/index.ts`:

```typescript
import * as yargs from 'yargs'; const argv = yargs.argv;
const checkWebsiteStatus = (url: string) => {
// ...existing code...
};
if (argv.url) { checkWebsiteStatus(argv.url);
} else {
console.error('Please provide a URL using --url argument.');
}
```

Run it with:

```bash
node dist/index.js --url https://www.example.com
```

2. Logging

To manage logging better, consider using a library like `winston`, which allows for customizable logging with different log levels.

3. Configuration Files

For more complex tools, you might want to incorporate configuration files (e.g., JSON or YAML) to encapsulate various settings.

Deploying Your CLI Tool

For easy distribution, you can publish your CLI tool to npm. Follow these steps:

Add a `bin` section to `package.json`:

```json "bin": {
"my-cli-tool": "./dist/index.js"
}
```

After compiling your project, link the package globally:

```bash npm link
```

You can now run your tool directly from anywhere:

```bash
my-cli-tool --url https://www.example.com
```

```
` ` `
```

We explored the process of building a CLI tool using TypeScript for DevOps automation. By leveraging TypeScript's static typing, we improved code quality and maintainability. You learned how to set up a project, write a simple CLI tool, enhance its functionality, and even prepare it for distribution.

Automating Server Configurations and Deployments with TypeScript

This chapter explores how TypeScript, a statically typed superset of JavaScript, can be effectively employed in automating server configurations and deployments. By leveraging TypeScript's features, including strong typing, interfaces, and advanced tooling, developers can create robust automation scripts that are both maintainable and easy to extend.

1. Understanding Server Configuration and Deployment

Before diving into automation techniques, it's essential to define what server configuration and deployment entail.

1.1 Server Configuration

Server configuration involves setting up the server environment to ensure that it can properly host and serve applications. This includes configuring server settings, installing necessary software, managing databases, and setting up network components such as firewalls or load balancers. The goal is to create a stable, secure, and optimized environment tailored to the application's needs.

1.2 Deployment

Deployment refers to the process of moving the application code from a development environment to a production environment. This process might involve transferring files, setting environment variables, and ensuring that all dependencies are satisfied. A successful deployment leads to an application that performs well in its production environment.

2. The Need for Automation

Manual configurations and deployments can be error-prone and time-consuming. Whenever adjustments need to be made, the risk of inconsistent environments increases, potentially leading to deployment failures or unexpected behavior in production. This is where automation comes into play:

Consistency: Automation ensures that configurations are applied uniformly across environments.

Efficiency: Automated processes can significantly reduce deployment times.

Version Control: Using code for configurations enables tracking changes and rollback capabilities.

Scalability: Automation makes it easier to scale applications and environments as demand grows. ## 3. Setting Up Your Environment

To get started with automating server configurations and deployments using TypeScript, you'll need to set up the right environment:

3.1 Prerequisites

Node.js: Ensure you have Node.js installed, as

TypeScript compiles down to JavaScript, which runs on Node.

TypeScript: Install TypeScript globally using npm:

```bash
npm install -g typescript
```

Development Tools: Choose a code editor that supports TypeScript (e.g., Visual Studio Code). ### 3.2 Initializing a TypeScript Project

To create a new TypeScript project, run the following commands:

```bash
mkdir server-automation cd server-automation npm init -y

npm install typescript ts-node @types/node --save-dev
npx tsc --init
```

This sets up a basic TypeScript project structure. ## 4. Automating Server Configurations

4.1 Defining Configuration Interfaces

One of the strengths of TypeScript is its ability to define strict interfaces. This is particularly useful when defining server configurations. You can start by creating an interface for your server configuration:

```typescript
```

```typescript
interface ServerConfig { hostname: string;
port: number; sslEnabled: boolean; databaseUrl: string;
}
```

4.2 Creating a Configuration Script

Next, create a configuration script that reads a configuration file and applies the settings. You might use a JSON file for this purpose.

```json
// config.json
{
"hostname": "localhost", "port": 8080, "sslEnabled": false,
"databaseUrl": "mongodb://localhost:27017/myapp"
}
```

```typescript
import * as fs from 'fs';
function loadConfig(): ServerConfig {
const rawData = fs.readFileSync('config.json', 'utf8');
return JSON.parse(rawData) as ServerConfig;
}
const config = loadConfig();
console.log(`Server will run on ${config.hostname}:${config.port}`);
```

```
```

4.3 Applying Server Configurations

Using libraries such as `child_process`, you can execute shell commands to apply your configurations dynamically. Here's an example:

```typescript

import { exec } from 'child_process';

exec(`echo "Configuring server at ${config.hostname} on port ${config.port}"`, (error, stdout, stderr) => { if (error)
{

console.error(`Error: ${error.message}`); return;

}

if (stderr) {

console.error(`Stderr: ${stderr}`); return;

}

console.log(stdout);

});
```
```

## 5. Automating Deployments ### 5.1 Deployment Scripting

The deployment process can also be automated using TypeScript. This includes tasks such as copying files to the server, updating environment variables, and restarting services.

```typescript

function deployApplication() {
```
```

```
exec('scp -r ./dist/* user@server:/path/to/deploy', (error,
stdout, stderr) => { if (error) {

console.error(`Deployment Error: ${error.message}`);
return;

}

if (stderr) {

console.error(`Deployment Stderr: ${stderr}`); return;

}

console.log(`Deployment Output: ${stdout}`);

});

}
```
```

### 5.2 Integrating with CI/CD

For a more sophisticated deployment process, consider integrating your TypeScript scripts with Continuous Integration/Continuous Deployment (CI/CD) tools like GitHub Actions, CircleCI, or Jenkins. This ensures that your configurations and deploys are executed automatically upon certain triggers (e.g., code pushes, pull requests).

By leveraging TypeScript's strong typing and advanced features, developers can create maintainable scripts that streamline operations. Embracing automation not only minimizes errors and reduces deployment time but also allows teams to focus on building great software, rather than wrestling with repetitive tasks.
```

Chapter 4: Building Robust CI/CD Pipelines with TypeScript

In this chapter, we will delve into how TypeScript can enhance the robustness of your CI/CD pipelines, providing you with a solid foundation to build and maintain high-quality applications.

4.1 Understanding CI/CD Basics

Before we dive into the specifics of using TypeScript, it's essential to grasp the basic concepts of CI and CD. ### 4.1.1 Continuous Integration

Continuous Integration is a software development practice where developers regularly merge their code changes into a central repository. Each merge is then automatically tested, ensuring that new code integrates well with the existing codebase. This practice helps to identify bugs early, improve software quality, and reduce integration problems.

4.1.2 Continuous Deployment

Continuous Deployment extends CI by automating the deployment of applications to production environments. Following rigorous automated testing, code changes that pass all tests are deployed without manual intervention. This ensures that new features and fixes reach users faster and with more frequency, which can greatly enhance user satisfaction.

4.2 Why TypeScript for CI/CD?

TypeScript is a superset of JavaScript that adds static typing, making it easier to catch errors during the development phase rather than at runtime. Incorporating

TypeScript into your CI/CD pipeline improves reliability and maintainability through:

Type Safety: Static type checking helps in discovering potential issues at compile time, reducing the likelihood of runtime errors.

Better Tooling: TypeScript comes with an extensive ecosystem of tools and IDE support, facilitating faster development and easier debugging.

Improved Documentation: The type system serves as a form of documentation, making it easier for teams to understand how to use different parts of the codebase.

4.3 Setting Up a TypeScript CI/CD Pipeline ### 4.3.1 Prerequisites

To get started with a TypeScript CI/CD pipeline, ensure you have the following tools installed:

Node.js & npm (or yarn)

TypeScript

A version control system (e.g., Git)

A CI/CD service (e.g., GitHub Actions, CircleCI, Travis CI) ### 4.3.2 Project Structure

Start with a simple TypeScript project. Here's a suggested folder structure:

```
` ` `

my-typescript-project/ src/

index.ts tests/

index.test.ts package.json tsconfig.json
```

.gitignore
```

In `package.json`, include the necessary scripts for building, testing, and linting your project:

```json
{
"scripts": { "build": "tsc",
"test": "jest",
"lint": "eslint ."
},
"devDependencies": { "typescript": "^4.0.0",
"jest": "^26.0.0",
"ts-jest": "^26.0.0",
"eslint": "^7.0.0",
"eslint-plugin-typescript": "^3.0.0"
}
}
```

4.3.3 Writing Tests

Testing is a crucial component of CI/CD. With TypeScript, you can use testing frameworks like Jest or Mocha. Here's a simple test case:

```typescript
// tests/index.test.ts
```
```

```
import { sum } from '../src';

test('adds 1 + 2 to equal 3', () => { expect(sum(1,
2)).toBe(3);

});
```

4.3.4 Configuring CI/CD

Now, let's set up GitHub Actions as our CI/CD provider.
Create a `.github/workflows/ci.yml` file in your
repository:

```yaml
name: CI

on:

push:

branches: [ main ] pull_request: branches: [ main ]

jobs:

build:

runs-on: ubuntu-latest steps:

uses: actions/checkout@v2

name: Set up Node.js

uses: actions/setup-node@v2 with:

node-version: '14'

name: Install dependencies run: npm install

name: Build

run: npm run build

name: Lint
```

```
run: npm run lint

name: Test

run: npm run test
```

4.3.5 Adding Deployment

To implement continuous deployment, modify your CI workflow to include deployment steps. For example, if you're deploying a Node.js application to Heroku:

```yaml
name: Deploy to Heroku

uses: akhileshns/heroku-deploy@v3.13.10 with:

heroku_api_key: ${{ secrets.HEROKU_API_KEY }}
heroku_app_name: 'your-app-name'

heroku_email: 'your-email@example.com'
```

4.4 Monitoring and Logging

Once your CI/CD pipeline is up and running, monitoring becomes essential. Ensure you have logging in place to track builds and deployments. Integrating tools like Sentry, Loggly, or even custom logging solutions can help pinpoint issues faster.

4.5 Best Practices

Keep Your Pipelines Simple: Avoid overly complex workflows. Use parallel jobs where beneficial, but ensure clarity.

Fail Fast: Configure your pipeline to fail at the earliest stage possible to save time and resources.

Automate Everything: From testing to deployment, the fewer manual processes you have, the better your pipeline will perform.

Regularly Review Your Pipeline: Continuous improvement should be a part of your culture. Regularly revisit your CI/CD processes to find areas for optimization.

By leveraging TypeScript's advantages of type safety and tool support, you can reduce errors, improve developer productivity, and ensure reliable software production.

Integrating TypeScript into Jenkins, GitHub Actions, and GitLab CI

TypeScript, a superset of JavaScript, has grown in popularity due to its robust type system and improved tooling capabilities. Integrating TypeScript into CI/CD pipelines using Jenkins, GitHub Actions, and GitLab CI can enhance the development workflow, ensuring that TypeScript code is linted, tested, and built consistently across multiple environments. In this chapter, we will explore how to seamlessly integrate TypeScript into these popular CI/CD platforms.

1. Prerequisites for Integration

Before diving into the integration process, it is crucial to set up your development environment with the following prerequisites:

Install Node.js and npm (Node Package Manager).

Ensure TypeScript is installed in your project (`npm install typescript --save-dev`).

(Optional) Use a linter like ESLint for static code analysis (`npm install eslint --save-dev`).

Set up unit tests using a framework like Jest (`npm install jest --save-dev`).

Having a well-structured project with a `tsconfig.json` file and defined scripts in `package.json` is also recommended for smooth integration.

2. Integrating TypeScript with Jenkins

2.1 Setting Up Your Jenkins Environment

Install Jenkins: If you haven't set up Jenkins yet, you can download it from [Jenkins' official site](https://www.jenkins.io/).

Install NodeJS Plugin: Go to Manage Jenkins > Manage Plugins > Available, and install the NodeJS Plugin.

Configure NodeJS: Go to Manage Jenkins > Global Tool Configuration, and add a NodeJS installation.

2.2 Creating a Jenkins Pipeline

You can create a Jenkins pipeline job that executes TypeScript-specific tasks.

```groovy
pipeline {

agent any

stages {

stage('Install Dependencies') { steps {
```

```
script {
sh 'npm install'
}
}
}
stage('Lint') {

steps {
script {
sh 'npx eslint .'
}
}
}
stage('Build') { steps {
script {
sh 'npx tsc'
}
}
}
stage('Test') { steps {
script {
sh 'npx jest'
}
```

```
}
}
}
}
```
\ \ \

This pipeline installs dependencies, lints the code, builds the TypeScript project, and runs tests, thereby validating the code in a CI environment.

3. Integrating TypeScript with GitHub Actions ### 3.1 Setting Up GitHub Actions

Create Workflow File: First, create a directory called `.github/workflows` in your repository and then create a `.yml` file for your workflow, for instance, `typescript-ci.yml`.

3.2 Sample GitHub Actions Workflow

Insert the following content into your `typescript-ci.yml` file:

```yaml
name: TypeScript CI

on:

push: branches:

main pull_request: branches:

main

jobs:

build:
```

```
runs-on: ubuntu-latest

steps:

name: Checkout code  uses: actions/checkout@v2


name: Setup Node.js

uses: actions/setup-node@v2 with:

node-version: '16'

name: Install Dependencies run: npm install


` ` `


name: Run ESLint run: npx eslint .

name: Build run: npx tsc

name: Run Tests run: npx jest
```

This workflow will trigger on every push or pull request to the `main` branch, ensuring that your TypeScript project is continually validated.

4. Integrating TypeScript with GitLab CI ### 4.1 Setting Up GitLab CI

GitLab CI utilizes a file named `.gitlab-ci.yml` that defines the CI/CD pipeline. ### 4.2 Sample GitLab CI Configuration

Create or edit the `.gitlab-ci.yml` file at the root of your repository:

```yaml
stages:
  install
  lint
  build
  test

install_dependencies:
  stage: install
  image: node:16
  script:
    npm install

lint:
  stage: lint
  image: node:16
  script:
    npx eslint .

build:
  stage: build
  image: node:16
  script:
    npx tsc

test:
  stage: test
  image: node:16
  script:
    npx jest
```

In this setup, each job runs in a Node.js Docker container, ensuring the environment is consistent. Each stage will run sequentially, providing clear visibility into where failures might occur.

Integrating TypeScript into Jenkins, GitHub Actions, and

GitLab CI offers a structured approach to maintain code quality and ensure code behavior remains consistent across environments. By leveraging pipelines in these CI/CD tools, developers can focus more on writing code while the automated processes manage the testing, linting, and building of their TypeScript projects.

Writing Custom CI/CD Scripts with TypeScript for Faster Deployments

In this chapter, we will explore how TypeScript can be employed to create custom CI/CD scripts that not only streamline deployments but also improve maintainability, readability, and type safety.

Understanding CI/CD and the Need for Customization

CI/CD practices typically involve several key stages:

Continuous Integration (CI): Developers merge their code changes into a shared repository

frequently, triggering automated builds and tests to identify issues early in the development cycle.

Continuous Deployment (CD): Following successful integrations, the code is automatically deployed to production or other environments.

While many CI/CD platforms like GitHub Actions, GitLab CI, and CircleCI offer built-in features and configurations, there are instances where specific workflows require tailored solutions. Here are some reasons why you might need custom CI/CD scripts:

Complex Deployment Requirements: Projects often have unique build processes, external service integrations, and environment configurations that standard templates can't address.

Enhanced Feedback: Custom scripts can provide better error handling and debugging information, allowing for quicker fixes and less downtime.

Increased Control: Custom solutions give you direct control over the deployment process, enabling you to optimize performance and resource utilization.

Type Safety and Tooling: By writing scripts in TypeScript, you can leverage its type system, making your scripts less error-prone and easier to maintain.

Setting Up TypeScript for CI/CD Scripting

Before diving into writing custom scripts, ensure you have a TypeScript environment set up. Follow the steps below to configure your project:

Initialize a Node.js project:

```bash
mkdir my-ci-scripts cd my-ci-scripts npm init -y
```

Install TypeScript:

```bash
npm install typescript --save-dev
```

Create a tsconfig.json file:

72

```bash
npx tsc --init
```

This file will contain TypeScript compiler options. Adjust settings as needed for your project.

Install additional dependencies:

Depending on your CI/CD needs, you may require other packages such as Axios for HTTP requests or dotenv for environment variable management:

```bash
npm install axios dotenv
```

Writing Your First CI/CD Script

Let's write a simple CI/CD script using TypeScript that performs the following tasks:

Builds the application.

Runs tests.

Deploys the application if the tests are successful.

Create a new file named `ci-cd-script.ts`:

```typescript
import { execSync } from 'child_process'; import * as dotenv from 'dotenv';

dotenv.config();

const BUILD_COMMAND = 'npm run build'; const
```

```
TEST_COMMAND = 'npm test';
const DEPLOY_COMMAND = 'npm run deploy';
function runCommand(command: string) { try {
console.log(`Executing:          ${command}`);
execSync(command, { stdio: 'inherit' });
} catch (error) {
console.error(`Error executing command: ${command}`);
process.exit(1);
}
}
function main() {
console.log('Starting CI/CD process...');
// Step 1: Build the application
runCommand(BUILD_COMMAND);
// Step 2: Run tests runCommand(TEST_COMMAND);
// Step 3: Deploy if tests pass
runCommand(DEPLOY_COMMAND);
console.log('CI/CD process completed successfully!');
}


main();
```

Explanation of the Script

Imports: We import `execSync` from the `child_process` module to execute shell commands and `dotenv` for environment variable management.

Command Constants: We define constants for the build, test, and deploy commands. These should align with your project's actual scripts in `package.json`.

runCommand Function: This function encapsulates the logic to execute a command. It logs the command being executed and handles errors gracefully, exiting the process if a command fails.

main Function: Clearly structured to perform the CI/CD steps sequentially: building the app, running tests, and deploying.

Running the Script

To run the script, ensure you have TypeScript compiled into JavaScript:

```bash
npx tsc
```

You'll find a compiled `ci-cd-script.js` file in your project directory (based on your `tsconfig.json` settings). Execute the script with Node.js:

```bash
node build/ci-cd-script.js
```

Integrating with Your CI/CD Platform

Once your script is tested locally, integrate it into your CI/CD pipeline. This generally involves adding the script execution command to your platform's configuration file—

like `.gitlab-ci.yml` for GitLab CI or
`.github/workflows/your-workflow.yml` for GitHub Actions. Example for GitHub Actions:

```yaml
name: CI/CD Pipeline
on:
push:
branches:
- main
jobs:
build:
runs-on: ubuntu-latest steps:
- name: Checkout code uses: actions/checkout@v2
```

name: Install Node.js

uses: actions/setup-node@v2 with:

node-version: '14'

name: Install dependencies run: npm install

name: Run CI/CD Script run: node build/ci-cd-script.js

Best Practices for CI/CD Scripts

Modularize Your Code: Consider breaking down your CI/CD scripts into smaller modules that handle specific functionalities, making it easier to read and maintain.

Use Environment Variables: Storing sensitive information and configuration in environment variables enhances security and flexibility.

Implement Error Handling: Ensure your scripts handle errors gracefully. This includes logging relevant information for debugging and cleaning up resources if necessary.

Optimize Performance: Profile your scripts and identify any bottlenecks. Make optimizations to reduce build times and improve overall efficiency.

Document Your Scripts: Well-documented scripts make it easier for team members to understand and maintain them in the long run.

By leveraging TypeScript's features—such as type safety and enhanced tooling—you can create robust and maintainable scripts tailored for your project's unique requirements. Whether you are automating build processes, running tests, or deploying to production, custom scripts offer unparalleled flexibility and control over your CI/CD pipeline.

Chapter 5: Securing DevOps Workflows with TypeScript

One of the key challenges is integrating security into the fast-paced, agile methodologies typical of DevOps. In this chapter, we will explore how TypeScript, a superset of JavaScript that adds static typing, can bolster security in DevOps workflows. We will examine best practices, tools, and methodologies that utilize TypeScript to secure the software development lifecycle effectively.

Understanding DevOps and the Security Imperative

DevOps aims to shorten the software development lifecycle while delivering features, fixes, and updates in alignment with business objectives. This cultural and professional movement emphasizes collaboration between development and operations teams. However, the rapid pace and high frequency of deployments can lead to vulnerabilities if security is not prioritized.

The Shift-Left Approach

To ensure security in DevOps workflows, organizations are adopting the "shift-left" approach. This approach emphasizes identifying and addressing security issues early in the development process, rather than waiting until later stages. By shifting left, teams can leverage automated testing, continuous integration (CI), and continuous deployment (CD) pipelines to catch vulnerabilities and design flaws earlier, making it easier to rectify issues before they reach production.

TypeScript: Enhancing Security in Development

TypeScript is designed to help developers write cleaner

and more maintainable code. By introducing static typing, TypeScript eliminates many common errors before runtime, which can lead to potential security vulnerabilities. Let's explore how TypeScript can be effectively utilized within DevOps workflows.

1. **Static Typing for Fewer Runtime Errors**

One of the primary benefits of TypeScript is its static type checking. Instead of relying solely on runtime validation, TypeScript allows developers to catch type-related errors during the development phase. This early detection can prevent issues such as type coercion vulnerabilities, which are common in JavaScript applications.

For instance, consider the following TypeScript code snippet:

```typescript
// Type assertion example
function processUserInput(input: string | null) {
// Using type checking to ensure 'input' is a string before proceeding if (input) {
console.log(`User input is: ${input}`);
} else {
console.error('No input provided');
}
}
```

By explicitly handling potential null values, developers can reduce the risk of unexpected behavior when handling user input.

2. **Improving Code Quality with Interfaces and Enums**

TypeScript allows for better code organization through the use of interfaces and enums. This organization leads to improved code readability and maintainability, making it easier to identify and patch potential security vulnerabilities.

For example:

```typescript
// Define an interface for user role interface User {

id: number; name: string; role: UserRole;

}

// Define an enum for user roles enum UserRole {

ADMIN = 'ADMIN', USER = 'USER',

}

// Function to get user permissions based on their role
function getUserPermissions(user: User): string[] {

switch (user.role) {

case UserRole.ADMIN:

return ['READ', 'WRITE', 'DELETE'];

case UserRole.USER: return ['READ'];

default:

return [];

}
```

```
}
```
```

This clear definition helps prevent unauthorized access by enforcing strict role-checking protocols. ### 3. **Using TypeScript with Security Libraries**

TypeScript seamlessly integrates with various security-focused libraries that can enrich your DevOps practices. Libraries such as `jsonwebtoken` for authentication and `express-validator` for input validation not only add security layers but also benefit from TypeScript's type-checking capabilities.

Here's a brief example of using `express-validator` with TypeScript:

```typescript
import { body, validationResult } from 'express-validator';
import express from 'express';

const app = express();

// Middleware to validate incoming data app.post('/user',
[

body('email').isEmail().withMessage('Invalid      email
format'),     body('password').isLength({     min:     5
}).withMessage('Password is too short')

], (req, res) => {

const errors = validationResult(req); if (!errors.isEmpty())
{

return res.status(400).json({ errors: errors.array() });

}
```
```

```
// Proceed with user registration...

});
` ` `
```

Using validation libraries helps to enforce input sanitization, thus protecting against common attacks such as SQL injection and cross-site scripting (XSS).

Integrating TypeScript into CI/CD Pipelines

Integrating TypeScript into CI/CD pipelines is essential for maintaining code quality and security. Tools like ESLint and Prettier can be configured to run as part of the CI process, enforcing coding standards and detecting vulnerabilities in TypeScript code before deployments reach production.

1. **Setting Up ESLint for TypeScript**

ESLint is an essential tool for identifying problematic patterns in code. By using TypeScript's parser, developers can ensure that code adheres to best practices while catching potential security vulnerabilities.

To set it up, include the following in your `.eslintrc.js` file:

```javascript
module.exports = {
parser: '@typescript-eslint/parser', extends: [
'eslint:recommended',                'plugin:@typescript-
eslint/recommended',
],
rules: {
// Custom rules for security
```

82

```
'no-eval': 'error', // Avoid evaluating strings as code

'prefer-const': 'warn', // Encourage use of const for
immutability

},

};
```
` ` `

2. **Running TypeScript Type Checks**

Automating TypeScript type checks as part of your build process ensures that type safety is maintained. For example, you could include a command in your CI pipeline to run `tsc --noEmit` to verify type correctness without generating output files.

` ` `yaml

Example GitHub Actions CI workflow snippet jobs:

build:

runs-on: ubuntu-latest steps:

uses: actions/checkout@v2

name: Install dependencies run: npm install

name: Run TypeScript checks run: npm run tsc --noEmit

name: Run tests run: npm test

` ` `

By embracing TypeScript's features—like static typing, interfaces, and rich ecosystem of security libraries—teams can adopt a "shift-left" approach to security. Incorporating TypeScript in CI/CD pipelines allows organizations to enforce security protocols while promoting agile development.

Implementing Security Best Practices in TypeScript Scripts

TypeScript, a superset of JavaScript, provides developers with strong typing and enhanced tooling, making it a popular choice for building complex applications. However, with the advantages of TypeScript come specific security challenges that must be addressed. This chapter explores the best practices for implementing security in TypeScript scripts, ensuring that your applications are robust, secure, and resilient against common vulnerabilities.

Understanding Security Threats

Before delving into specific best practices, it is essential to understand the various security threats that your TypeScript applications might face:

Injection Attacks: These include SQL injection, command injection, and cross-site scripting (XSS), where malicious input is executed by the application.

Data Exposure: Sensitive information may be exposed due to inadequate data protection measures, such as improper handling of user credentials.

Cross-Site Request Forgery (CSRF): An attack that tricks a user into unknowingly submitting requests that can change their state in an application.

Insecure Dependencies: Utilizing third-party libraries that have known vulnerabilities can introduce security risks to your application.

Improper Error Handling: Allowing application errors to reveal sensitive information to users could lead to exploitation.

Security Best Practices for TypeScript ### 1. Use Type Safety to Validate Input

TypeScript's strong typing system helps developers validate input effectively. Define interfaces and types for any data structures you're working with. Always check that incoming data conforms to these structures:

```typescript
interface User {

id: number; name: string; email: string;

}

function createUser(user: User): void {

// Business logic

}
```

This approach ensures that data meets the expected format before further processing, minimizing the risk of injection attacks.

2. Sanitize User Inputs

Even when you are leveraging TypeScript's type safety, it's crucial to sanitize inputs to protect against XSS and other injection attacks.

Use libraries like `DOMPurify` when dealing with HTML

strings:

```typescript
import DOMPurify from 'dompurify';

const userComment: string = getUserComment(); // Simulated user input const safeComment = DOMPurify.sanitize(userComment);
```

3. Implement Strong Authentication & Authorization

Utilizing robust security measures for user authentication and authorization is vital. Implement token-based authentication (e.g., JWT) for stateless sessions. Always ensure that user roles are verified before allowing access to sensitive operations:

```typescript
function isAdmin(user: User): boolean { return user.role === 'admin';
}

// Middleware to protect routes

function adminOnly(req: Request, res: Response, next: NextFunction) { if (!isAdmin(req.user)) {

return res.status(403).send('Forbidden');

}

next();

}
```

4. Manage Dependencies Wisely

Regularly update your dependencies to minimize exposure to known vulnerabilities. Utilize tools like `npm audit` or `Snyk` to check for insecure packages. Lock versions in `package.json` to stabilize the environment:

```json
"dependencies": {
"express": "^4.17.1"
}
```

5. Employ Secure Coding Practices Adopt secure coding principles such as:

Least Privilege: Grant only the necessary permissions required to achieve functionality.

Fail Securely: Design your application to fail without revealing sensitive information.

Use HTTPS: Always encrypt data in transit by serving your application over HTTPS. ### 6. Handle Errors Carefully

Implement proper error handling mechanisms to avoid leaking sensitive information:

```typescript
app.use((err: Error, req: Request, res: Response, next: NextFunction) => { console.error(err); // Log error for debugging res.status(500).send('Something went wrong!');
});
```

Keep detailed error logs for developers but display generic

messages to end users. ### 7. Secure APIs

For applications consuming APIs, ensure that sensitive data is transmitted safely:

Utilize OAuth 2.0 for secure API access.

Validate API request payloads thoroughly.

Implement rate limiting to prevent abuse of your APIs. ### 8. Continuous Security Testing

Establish automated security testing processes within your CI/CD pipeline. Introduce static code analysis tools such as `ESLint` with security-specific rules, and consider dynamic testing tools for runtime vulnerabilities.

By understanding potential security threats and adopting a proactive mindset towards security, developers can create applications that not only function efficiently but also protect user data and maintain trust.

Detecting Vulnerabilities with Static Analysis and TypeScript Linters

In this environment, security vulnerabilities can not only compromise sensitive data but also damage a company's reputation and incite financial losses. One of the most effective methods for uncovering these vulnerabilities early in the development cycle is through static analysis combined with the power of TypeScript linters. This chapter delves into the principles of static analysis, the advantages of TypeScript for building robust applications, and the tools and best practices that can aid developers in detecting vulnerabilities before they reach production.

Understanding Static Analysis

Static analysis refers to the process of examining code without executing it. Unlike dynamic analysis, which tests the execution of a program in real-time, static analysis offers insights into potential flaws in code structure and logic at an early stage. By reviewing the program's source code, tooling can identify vulnerabilities such as:

Syntax errors

Type inconsistencies

Code smells

Security vulnerabilities

One of the primary advantages of static analysis is its ability to catch issues at compile-time rather than run-time, thus reducing the likelihood of encountering bugs in production.

The Role of TypeScript

TypeScript enhances JavaScript by introducing strong typing and other features that promote cleaner code. As developers strive for maintainability and safety, TypeScript's static typing minimizes the risk of errors. For instance, if a developer tries to assign a string value to a variable that should hold a number, TypeScript will throw an error during compilation, alerting the developer before the code runs.

In addition to type safety, TypeScript brings several features that aid in identifying vulnerabilities, including:

Interfaces and Types: Define clear contracts for objects, making it easier to reason about data flows and reducing the risk of vulnerabilities that stem from improper data handling.

Enums: Help prevent invalid values from being used in your code, thereby reducing bugs related to invalid states.

Strict Mode: By enabling the strict mode, developers can catch errors that might go unnoticed, such as

`null` or `undefined` assignments.

TypeScript Linters for Vulnerability Detection

Linters are essential development tools that analyze code for stylistic errors, potential bugs, and insecure coding practices. In the context of TypeScript, linters like ESLint can be configured to extend beyond traditional code style checks to improve security.

ESLint and TSLint

Though TSLint was the original linter specifically designed for TypeScript, it has since been deprecated in favor of ESLint, which now supports TypeScript through plugins. Here's how to set up and utilize ESLint to spot vulnerabilities:

Installing ESLint:

To get started, you need to install ESLint and its TypeScript parser. This can be done using npm:

```bash
npm install eslint @typescript-eslint/parser @typescript-eslint/eslint-plugin --save-dev
```

Configuring ESLint:

Create a configuration file (`.eslintrc.js`) in your project root:

```javascript
module.exports = {
parser: '@typescript-eslint/parser', extends: [
'eslint:recommended',                    'plugin:@typescript-eslint/recommended',
],
rules: {
'no-unused-vars': 'warn',
'@typescript-eslint/no-explicit-any': 'warn',
// Additional rules to catch security-related patterns
},
};
```

Running ESLint:

You can integrate ESLint into your build process or run it manually:

```bash
npx eslint 'src/**/*.ts'
```

Best Practices for Detecting Vulnerabilities

To maximize the effectiveness of static analysis and linters for vulnerability detection, consider implementing these best practices:

Regularly Update Your Tools: Tools evolve to address

new vulnerabilities and coding practices. Regular updates ensure that you benefit from the latest security fixes and enhancements.

Implement Continuous Integration (CI): Integrate static analysis into your CI pipeline. This way, issues can be detected automatically during every commit or pull request, allowing for swift remediation.

Customize Security Rules: Adapt the configuration of your linter to focus on secure coding practices that are particularly relevant to your application domain. This might include avoiding the use of `eval`, validating input, and prohibiting the use of insecure libraries.

Educate Your Team: Conduct training sessions on common security vulnerabilities like SQL injection, Cross-Site Scripting (XSS), and improper error handling. A well-informed team is instrumental in preventing vulnerabilities before they manifest.

Code Reviews: Pair static analysis tools with manual code reviews. While linters can automate much of the detection, human insight remains crucial in identifying complex vulnerabilities that tools may miss.

Detecting vulnerabilities through static analysis and TypeScript linters is a proactive approach that strengthens the security posture of software applications. By leveraging TypeScript's robust type system and integrating tools like ESLint into the development workflow, organizations can catch potential issues early, fostering a culture of security and maintainability.

Chapter 6: TypeScript for Cloud Automation

TypeScript, a statically typed superset of JavaScript, offers a unique combination of features that make it an ideal language for cloud automation. In this chapter, we will explore how TypeScript can be leveraged for cloud automation, covering various tools, practices, and real-world examples.

1. Why TypeScript for Cloud Automation? ### 1.1 Type Safety

One of the primary advantages of TypeScript is its type system. Type safety helps catch potential errors at compile time rather than at runtime, which is especially crucial in cloud environments where bugs can lead to significant downtime, increased costs, or data loss. By using TypeScript, developers can define clear interfaces, ensuring that different components of a cloud automation pipeline work seamlessly together.

1.2 Familiarity and Versatility

Since TypeScript compiles down to JavaScript, it is compatible with a wide variety of platforms and libraries commonly used in cloud environments. Developers familiar with JavaScript can transition to TypeScript seamlessly, leveraging existing knowledge while gaining the benefits of a type-safe language.

1.3 Advanced Features

TypeScript includes many modern language features such as async/await, decorators, and interfaces, which facilitate the creation of complex automation scripts. These features enable developers to write more expressive and organized code, improving maintainability and readability.

2. Setting Up the Environment

To start using TypeScript for cloud automation, you'll need to set up your development environment. Here's a step-by-step guide:

2.1 Installing TypeScript

You can install TypeScript globally on your machine using npm:

```bash

npm install -g typescript

```

2.2 Initializing a Project

Once TypeScript is installed, initialize a new project by creating a directory and running:

```bash npm init -y tsc --init

```

This will create a `tsconfig.json` file where you can configure TypeScript options according to your project's needs.

2.3 Installing Necessary Libraries

To interact with cloud providers, you'll commonly use SDKs or libraries. For instance:

- For AWS, you can install the AWS SDK:

```bash

npm install aws-sdk
```

```
```

- For Azure, you may want the Azure SDK:

```bash
npm install @azure/storage-blob
```

3. Building Automation Scripts

3.1 Creating an AWS Lambda Function

AWS Lambda is a powerful service for running code in the cloud without provisioning servers. Here's how you can automate a simple Lambda function using TypeScript:

Create a new TypeScript file (e.g., `lambdaFunction.ts`):

```typescript
import { APIGatewayEvent, Context, Callback } from 'aws-lambda';

export const handler = async (event: APIGatewayEvent, context: Context, callback: Callback) => {
console.log('Received event:', JSON.stringify(event, null, 2));

return {

statusCode: 200,

body: JSON.stringify({ message: 'Hello from TypeScript Lambda!' })

};

};
```

Compile the TypeScript code:

```bash

tsc lambdaFunction.ts

```

Deploy the generated JavaScript code to AWS Lambda using the AWS CLI or the AWS Management Console.

3.2 Automating Cloud Resources with Terraform

Terraform is a popular infrastructure-as-code tool that can be programmatically managed with TypeScript. Using the `cdktf` (Cloud Development Kit for Terraform) allows you to define your infrastructure using TypeScript:

Install cdktf:

```bash

npm install cdktf

```

Define infrastructure in TypeScript:

```typescript

import { Construct } from 'constructs'; import { App, TerraformStack } from 'cdktf';

import { AwsProvider, S3Bucket } from './.gen/providers/aws';

class MyStack extends TerraformStack { constructor(scope: Construct, id: string) {

super(scope, id);

new AwsProvider(this, 'AWS', { region: 'us-west-2',
```

```
});
new S3Bucket(this, 'MyBucket', { bucket: 'my-awesome-bucket', acl: 'private',
});
}
}
const app = new App();
new MyStack(app, 'my-stack'); app.synth();
```

Deploy your stack:

```bash
cdktf deploy
```

4. Best Practices for Cloud Automation with TypeScript
4.1 Modularize Code

When working on cloud automation scripts, it's essential to keep your code modular. Break down your code into reusable components, making it easier to maintain and test.

4.2 Leverage Type Definitions

Use TypeScript type definitions for third-party libraries where available. This adds an additional layer of type safety and helps document your code as you develop.

4.3 Write Unit Tests

Automate your testing using frameworks like Jest. Writing unit tests for your cloud automation scripts helps catch errors early and ensures that your code behaves as expected.

4.4 Follow Cloud Provider's Best Practices

Each cloud provider has its own set of best practices for automation. Familiarize yourself with these to ensure your automation scripts are efficient, secure, and cost-effective.

By combining the advantages of TypeScript with popular cloud services and frameworks, developers can create robust automation solutions that enhance their cloud infrastructure's agility and reliability. In an evolving technological landscape, mastering TypeScript for cloud automation can position you and your organization for greater success in the realm of cloud computing.

Managing AWS, Azure, and Google Cloud with TypeScript SDKs

TypeScript, a superset of JavaScript, has gained popularity due to its strong typing, modern features, and outstanding tooling support, making it an excellent choice for interfacing with cloud SDKs.

This chapter explores how to manage cloud resources on AWS, Azure, and Google Cloud using TypeScript SDKs. We will cover the setup, key features of each SDK, fundamental tasks for managing resources, and best practices for multi-cloud management.

Setting Up TypeScript for Cloud Management

Before diving into the specifics of each cloud SDK, let's begin with the steps to set up a TypeScript project. ### 1. Install TypeScript

First, ensure you have Node.js and npm installed. Then, install TypeScript globally:

```bash
npm install -g typescript
```

2. Create a New Project

To create a new TypeScript project, run the following commands:

```bash
mkdir cloud-management cd cloud-management npm init -y

tsc --init
```

3. Install Cloud SDKs

Next, install the required SDKs. Below are the commands for the AWS SDK, Azure SDK, and Google Cloud SDK:

```bash
# AWS SDK
npm install aws-sdk
# Azure SDK
npm install @azure/identity @azure/storage-blob
# Google Cloud SDK
npm install @google-cloud/storage
```

4. Configure TypeScript

In your `tsconfig.json`, ensure the compiler options are set up correctly:

```json
{
"compilerOptions": { "target": "ES6", "module": "commonjs", "strict": true, "esModuleInterop": true, "skipLibCheck": true
}
}
```

Managing AWS Resources with TypeScript

Amazon Web Services (AWS) offers a powerful SDK that allows developers to manage cloud resources effectively. The AWS SDK for JavaScript, which is compatible with TypeScript, provides access to various services such as S3, EC2, Lambda, and more.

Initializing the AWS SDK

```typescript
import AWS from 'aws-sdk';

AWS.config.update({ region: 'us-west-2',

accessKeyId: 'YOUR_ACCESS_KEY_ID',
secretAccessKey: 'YOUR_SECRET_ACCESS_KEY',

});
```

Example: Managing S3 Buckets Creating a new S3 bucket:

```typescript
const s3 = new AWS.S3();

const createBucket = async (bucketName: string) => {
const params = {

Bucket: bucketName, ACL: 'public-read',

};

try {

await                s3.createBucket(params).promise();
console.log(`Bucket created: ${bucketName}`);

} catch (error) {

console.error(`Error creating bucket: ${error.message}`);

}

};


createBucket('my-new-bucket');
```

Managing Azure Resources with TypeScript

Microsoft Azure provides a set of SDKs to manage cloud services efficiently. The Azure SDK for JavaScript, which also supports TypeScript, helps developers interact with Azure resources seamlessly.

Initializing the Azure SDK

```typescript
```

```typescript
import { BlobServiceClient } from '@azure/storage-blob';

const AZURE_STORAGE_CONNECTION_STRING = 'YOUR_AZURE_STORAGE_CONNECTION_STRING';

const blobServiceClient = BlobServiceClient.fromConnectionString(AZURE_STORAGE_CONNECTION_STRING);
```

Example: Creating a New Blob Container
```typescript
const createBlobContainer = async (containerName: string) => {

const containerClient = blobServiceClient.getContainerClient(containerName);

try {

await containerClient.create(); console.log(`Container created: ${containerName}`);

} catch (error) {

console.error(`Error creating container: ${error.message}`);

}

};

createBlobContainer('my-new-container');
```

Managing Google Cloud Resources with TypeScript

Google Cloud Platform (GCP) offers an extensive set of services, and its SDK for JavaScript allows seamless interaction with these services.

Initializing the Google Cloud Storage Client

```typescript
import { Storage } from '@google-cloud/storage';

const storage = new Storage({ projectId: 'YOUR_PROJECT_ID',
keyFilename: 'path/to/your/keyfile.json',
});
```

Example: Creating a New GCS Bucket

```typescript
const createBucket = async (bucketName: string) => { try {

const [bucket] = await storage.createBucket(bucketName);
console.log(`Bucket created: ${bucket.name}`);
} catch (error) {

console.error(`Error creating bucket: ${error.message}`);
}
};
createBucket('my-new-gcs-bucket');
```

Best Practices for Multi-Cloud Management

Managing services across AWS, Azure, and Google Cloud

can be challenging, but with best practices, it becomes manageable:

Consistent Naming Conventions: Adopt a consistent naming convention for resources across all clouds to simplify resource identification.

Centralized Configuration Management: Utilize tools such as AWS Systems Manager Parameter Store, Azure App Configuration, or Google Cloud Secret Manager to manage configurations centrally.

Infrastructure as Code (IaC): Tools like Terraform can be invaluable for defining infrastructure across multiple clouds in a single configuration language.

Monitoring and Logging: Implement centralized logging and monitoring using tools like Datadog or Grafana, ensuring that you have visibility across all platforms.

Security Practices: Ensure IAM roles are appropriately set up and segregated by project needs; regularly audit permissions in all cloud environments.

Managing cloud resources across AWS, Azure, and Google Cloud using TypeScript SDKs can greatly streamline your development workflow. By understanding the distinct features of each SDK and how they interconnect, developers can create robust multi-cloud applications more efficiently. Through employing best practices, teams can mitigate potential pitfalls of multi-cloud operations, ultimately leading to a harmonious cloud experience.

Building Infrastructure as Code (IaC) with TypeScript and Pulumi

Traditional infrastructure management methods are often labor-intensive and prone to human error, leading to inconsistencies and inefficiencies. To address these challenges, Infrastructure as Code (IaC) has emerged as a transformative approach, allowing developers and operations teams to manage their infrastructure using code. In this chapter, we will explore how to implement IaC using TypeScript and Pulumi, a modern open-source tool designed for building cloud infrastructure.

1. Understanding Infrastructure as Code (IaC)

Before diving into the specifics of TypeScript and Pulumi, it's essential to understand the core principles of Infrastructure as Code. IaC allows you to define and manage your infrastructure through code, enabling you to:

Automate Configuration: Eliminate manual intervention by automating the provisioning and configuration of resources.

Version Control: Track changes to your infrastructure over time using version control systems like Git.

Consistency and Repeatability: Ensure that your environments are consistent each time they are deployed, reducing variability.

Collaboration and Transparency: Enable teams to collaborate more effectively with shared infrastructure codebases.

IaC can be implemented through various tools and

languages, including Terraform, CloudFormation, and Ansible. In this chapter, we will specifically focus on Pulumi, a tool that leverages traditional programming languages, including TypeScript, for defining infrastructure.

2. Introduction to Pulumi

Pulumi is a modern infrastructure as code framework that allows developers to use familiar programming languages to define cloud resources and workflows. With Pulumi, you can leverage the full power of programming constructs such as classes, functions, and loops, providing you with greater flexibility and expressiveness compared to declarative syntax alone.

Benefits of Using Pulumi

Familiar Development Experience: Integration with languages like TypeScript allows developers to utilize existing skills and tools.

Rich Ecosystem Support: Pulumi supports a wide range of cloud providers, including AWS, Azure, Google Cloud, Kubernetes, and more.

State Management: Pulumi maintains the state of your infrastructure seamlessly and efficiently.

Cross-Cloud Compatibility: Use a single language to manage infrastructure across multiple cloud providers.

3. Setting Up Your Environment

Before starting to build infrastructure using TypeScript and Pulumi, we need to set up our development environment. Here's how:

Prerequisites

Node.js: Ensure you have Node.js installed on your machine (at least version 14).

Pulumi: Install the Pulumi CLI by following the instructions on the [Pulumi installation page](https://www.pulumi.com/docs/get-started/install/).

Step-by-Step Installation

Install Pulumi CLI:

```bash

brew install pulumi # On macOS

# For Linux, use the appropriate package manager or download from the website
```

Verify Installation:

```bash

pulumi version
```

Create a new Pulumi project:

```bash

mkdir my-infra-project cd my-infra-project pulumi new typescript
```

This command will prompt you to provide a name for your project, a description, and the desired cloud provider. After answering the prompts, you will have a new Pulumi project set up with TypeScript.

4. Defining Infrastructure with TypeScript

Now that we have our environment set up, let's dive into creating our first infrastructure deployment. We will provision a simple cloud service, such as an AWS S3 bucket, as an example.

Creating an S3 Bucket

Open the `index.ts` file generated by Pulumi, and replace its contents with the following code:

```typescript
import * as pulumi from "@pulumi/pulumi"; import * as aws from "@pulumi/aws";

// Create an S3 bucket

const bucket = new aws.s3.Bucket("my-bucket", { acl: "private",

});

// Export the bucket name

export const bucketName = bucket.id;
```

Breakdown of the Code

Importing Libraries: We import Pulumi and the AWS library for defining AWS resources.

Creating an S3 Bucket: We create an S3 bucket using Pulumi's `aws.s3.Bucket` method.

Exporting Outputs: We export the bucket name so it can be easily referenced after the deployment. ## 5. Deploying Your Infrastructure

With your infrastructure code in place, it's time to deploy it to the cloud. ### Deploying with Pulumi

Run the following command in your project directory:

```bash
bash pulumi up
```

This command analyzes your project, displays a preview of the changes it will make, and prompts for your approval. If everything looks good, type `yes` to proceed with the deployment. Pulumi will create the resources defined in your TypeScript file.

Verifying the Deployment

Once the deployment is complete, you can verify that your S3 bucket has been created by logging into the AWS Management Console. You should see the newly created bucket listed under the S3 service.

6. Managing Infrastructure Changes

One of the biggest advantages of Infrastructure as Code is the ability to manage changes efficiently. Let's say you want to make some modifications, such as enabling versioning on your S3 bucket. You can accomplish this by updating your `index.ts` file:

```typescript
const bucket = new aws.s3.Bucket("my-bucket", { acl: "private",

versioning: { enabled: true,
},
});
```

109

```
```

After making the changes, run `pulumi up` again to apply the new configuration. Pulumi will determine the necessary changes and prompt you to confirm before executing them.

7. Cleaning Up Resources

Once you're done experimenting with your infrastructure, it's important to clean up and remove the resources you've created to avoid incurring unnecessary costs.

To destroy the infrastructure, run the following command:

```bash
pulumi destroy
```

You will be prompted to confirm the destruction of the resources. Type `yes` to proceed.

We covered the fundamentals of IaC, set up a development environment, defined our infrastructure, deployed it to the cloud, managed changes, and cleaned up resources. By leveraging TypeScript's features and Pulumi's capabilities, you can build and manage cloud infrastructure efficiently and effectively.

Chapter 7: TypeScript for API and Microservices Automation

TypeScript, with its strong typing and modern features, offers a compelling solution for developing and automating these API and microservices architectures. In this chapter, we will explore how to leverage TypeScript for automating interactions with APIs and microservices, emphasizing its benefits and providing practical examples to illustrate the concepts.

7.1 Understanding the Role of APIs and Microservices

APIs (Application Programming Interfaces) allow different software applications and services to communicate with one another. When architected as microservices, applications are divided into smaller, independent units that each handle specific business capabilities. This modular approach facilitates easier scaling, deployment, and maintenance.

7.1.1 The Benefits of Microservices

Scalability: Each service can be deployed and scaled independently.

Flexibility: Different services can be built with different technologies.

Resilience: Failure in one service does not affect the others. ### 7.1.2 The Role of APIs in Microservices

APIs serve as the communication layer between microservices, defining how they interact. RESTful APIs are particularly popular due to their stateless nature and use of standard HTTP protocols.

7.2 Why TypeScript?

TypeScript is a statically typed superset of JavaScript that compiles to plain JavaScript. Its strong typing, interfaces, and other modern features make it well-suited for large codebases, such as those found in microservices architectures.

7.2.1 Advantages of Using TypeScript for Microservices

Type Safety: Reduces runtime errors by catching typing issues at compile time.

Enhanced Developer Experience: Tools like IDEs provide better autocompletion and refactoring support.

Interoperability: Can work seamlessly with existing JavaScript libraries and frameworks. ## 7.3 Setting Up a TypeScript Project for Microservices

Before diving into coding, it's essential to set up a TypeScript project. Here's a step-by-step guide: ### 7.3.1 Initializing the Project

Install Node.js: Ensure you have Node.js installed.

Create a new directory:

```bash
mkdir my-microservice cd my-microservice
```

Initialize a new Node.js project:
```bash npm init -y
```

```
```

Install TypeScript:
```bash
npm install typescript --save-dev
```

Create a TypeScript configuration file:
```bash
npx tsc --init
```

7.3.2 Project Structure

Organizing the codebase is crucial for maintainability. A typical microservice structure could look as follows:
```
my-microservice/

src/
controllers/ routes/ services/ models/ index.ts

tests/

tsconfig.json package.json
```

7.4 Building a Simple REST API with TypeScript ### 7.4.1 Installing Necessary Dependencies

For creating a RESTful API, we will use Express.js. Let's install the required packages:

```bash
npm install express @types/express body-parser
```

7.4.2 Creating the API

Here's a simple example of a Todo API:

src/models/Todo.ts

```typescript
export interface Todo { id: number;
title: string; completed: boolean;
}
```

src/controllers/TodoController.ts

```typescript
import { Request, Response } from 'express'; import { Todo } from '../models/Todo';
let todos: Todo[] = []; let currentId = 1;
export const getTodos = (req: Request, res: Response) => { res.json(todos);
};
export const addTodo = (req: Request, res: Response) => { const { title } = req.body;
const newTodo: Todo = { id: currentId++, title, completed: false }; todos.push(newTodo);
```

```typescript
  res.status(201).json(newTodo);
};
```

src/routes/todoRoutes.ts

```typescript
import { Router } from 'express';
import { getTodos, addTodo } from '../controllers/TodoController'; const router = Router();
router.get('/todos', getTodos); router.post('/todos', addTodo);
export default router;
```

src/index.ts

```typescript
import express from 'express';
import bodyParser from 'body-parser';
import todoRoutes from './routes/todoRoutes';
const app = express(); const PORT = 3000;
app.use(bodyParser.json()); app.use('/api', todoRoutes);
app.listen(PORT, () => {
console.log(`Server is running on http://localhost:${PORT}`);
});
```

7.5 Automating Microservices with TypeScript ### 7.5.1 Interacting with Other APIs

TypeScript can be used to automate communication with external microservices or APIs. The Axios library is excellent for making HTTP requests.

Installing Axios

```bash
npm install axios @types/axios
```

Example: Fetch Todos from External API

```typescript
import axios from 'axios';

async function fetchTodos() { try {

const response = await axios.get('https://jsonplaceholder.typicode.com/todos');
return response.data;

} catch (error) {

console.error('Error fetching todos:', error);

}

}
```

7.5.2 Error Handling and Retry Logic

When dealing with multiple microservices, it's vital to implement error handling and possibly a retry mechanism. Here's how you might handle errors when making requests:

116

```typescript
async function fetchWithRetry(url: string, retries: number
= 3) { for (let i = 0; i < retries; i++) {

try {

const response = await axios.get(url); return
response.data;

} catch (error) {

if (i === retries - 1) {

console.error('Failed after multiple retries:', error); throw
error;

}

}

}

}
```

7.6 Testing Your Microservice

Testing is critical in microservices to ensure that each
service operates as expected. You can use Jest or Mocha
for testing your TypeScript microservices.

7.6.1 Setting Up Jest

```bash
npm install --save-dev jest ts-jest @types/jest npx ts-jest
config:init
```

7.6.2 Writing Tests

tests/todoController.test.ts

```typescript
import request from 'supertest'; import express from 'express';

import { addTodo, getTodos } from '../src/controllers/TodoController';

const app = express(); app.use(express.json()); app.get('/todos', getTodos); app.post('/todos', addTodo);

describe('Todo API', () => {

it('should fetch an empty array of todos', async () => { const response = await request(app).get('/todos'); expect(response.status).toBe(200); expect(response.body).toEqual([]);

});

it('should add a new todo', async () => {

const response = await request(app).post('/todos').send({ title: 'Test Todo' }); expect(response.status).toBe(201);

expect(response.body.title).toBe('Test Todo');

});

});
```

TypeScript is an excellent choice for automating APIs and microservices due to its rich feature set and type safety. In this chapter, we explored how to build a simple REST API with Express, interact with external APIs, and implement testing strategies. By leveraging TypeScript, developers can create robust, maintainable microservices that are easier to scale and manage.

Creating and Managing RESTful and GraphQL APIs with TypeScript

Two of the most popular architectural styles for building APIs are REST (Representational State Transfer) and GraphQL. Both approaches have their unique strengths and weaknesses, making them suitable for different use cases. In this chapter, we'll explore how to create and manage RESTful and GraphQL APIs using TypeScript—a powerful superset of JavaScript that provides static typing, interfaces, and better tooling.

We'll begin by setting up our environment and creating a simple RESTful API with TypeScript. Next, we will transition to building a GraphQL API and discuss how both can be effectively managed and maintained. Let's dive in!

Setting Up the Environment ### 1. Prerequisites

Before we begin, ensure you have the following installed:

Node.js (latest LTS version)

npm or yarn

TypeScript

A code editor (like Visual Studio Code) ### 2. Initializing a TypeScript Project

To create our project, start by creating a new directory and initializing a Node.js project:

```bash
```

```
mkdir my-api-project cd my-api-project npm init -y
```
```

Next, install TypeScript and the necessary type definitions:

```bash
npm install typescript ts-node @types/node --save-dev
```

Create a `tsconfig.json` file to configure TypeScript:

```json
{
"compilerOptions": { "target": "ESNext", "module": "CommonJS", "strict": true, "esModuleInterop": true,
"forceConsistentCasingInFileNames": true,

"skipLibCheck": true, "outDir": "./dist"
},
"include": ["src/**/*"],
"exclude": ["node_modules", "**/*.spec.ts"]
}
```

3. Creating a Basic RESTful API

We'll use Express, a minimalist web framework for Node.js, to create our RESTful API. Install Express and its type definitions:
```

```bash
npm install express
npm install @types/express --save-dev
```

Create a new folder called `src` and inside it, create an `index.ts` file. This file will act as our API's entry point.

```typescript
// src/index.ts
import express, { Request, Response } from 'express';
const app = express(); const PORT = 3000;
// Middleware to parse JSON bodies
app.use(express.json());
// Sample data for our API
let users: { id: number; name: string }[] = [
{ id: 1, name: 'Alice' },
{ id: 2, name: 'Bob' }
];
// RESTful endpoint to get all users app.get('/users', (req:
Request, res: Response) => { res.json(users);
});
// RESTful endpoint to get a user by ID
app.get('/users/:id', (req: Request, res: Response) => {
const user = users.find(u => u.id ===
parseInt(req.params.id)); if (user) {
res.json(user);
```

```
} else {

res.status(404).send('User not found');

}

});

// RESTful endpoint to create a new user
app.post('/users', (req: Request, res: Response) => {

const newUser = { id: users.length + 1, name:
req.body.name }; users.push(newUser);

res.status(201).json(newUser);

});

// Start the server app.listen(PORT, () => {

console.log(`Server          is          running          at
http://localhost:${PORT}`);

});
```
` ` `

4. Running the RESTful API

Compile and run your TypeScript code with:

```bash
npx ts-node src/index.ts
```

You can test the API endpoints using a tool like Postman or CURL. The endpoints allow you to manage users by listing them, retrieving a specific user, and adding a new user.

Transitioning to GraphQL

122

While REST APIs follow a fixed set of endpoints, GraphQL allows clients to request exactly the data they need, making API calls more efficient. In this section, we will create a GraphQL API using Apollo Server and TypeScript.

1. Installing Apollo Server

To create our GraphQL API, we will use Apollo Server:

```bash
npm install apollo-server graphql

npm install @types/graphql --save-dev
```

2. Creating the GraphQL API

In the `src` folder, create a new file called `graphql.ts`. This file will define our GraphQL schema and resolvers.

```typescript
// src/graphql.ts
import { ApolloServer, gql } from 'apollo-server';
// Sample data
let users: { id: number; name: string }[] = [
{ id: 1, name: 'Alice' },
{ id: 2, name: 'Bob' }
];
// GraphQL schema const typeDefs = gql`

type User { id: Int!
```

123

```
  name: String!
}
type Query { users: [User]!
user(id: Int!): User
}
type Mutation { createUser(name: String!): User
}
`;
// Resolvers
const resolvers = { Query: {
users: () => users,
user: (_: any, { id }: { id: number }) => users.find(u =>
u.id === id)
},
Mutation: {
createUser: (_: any, { name }: { name: string }) => { const
newUser  =  {  id:  users.length  +  1,  name };
users.push(newUser);
return newUser;
}
}
};
// Apollo Server
const server = new ApolloServer({ typeDefs, resolvers });
```

```
// Start the server server.listen().then(({ url }) => {
console.log(`???? Server ready at ${url}`);
});
```

3. Running the GraphQL API

Compile and run your new GraphQL server the same way you did with the REST API:

```bash
npx ts-node src/graphql.ts
```

You can test your GraphQL API using Apollo Studio or an equivalent GraphQL playground. With the above setup, we can query users and create new users.

Managing Your APIs ### 1. Documentation

Whether you choose REST or GraphQL, documenting your API is crucial. Use tools like Swagger (for REST) or GraphQL Playground (for GraphQL) to help describe your endpoints and functionality.

2. Versioning

APIs should be versioned to manage changes without breaking existing clients. For RESTful APIs, you can include the version in your endpoint URLs (e.g., `/v1/users`). In GraphQL, consider versioning your schema and maintaining backward compatibility.

3. Security

In both architectures, securing your API is paramount. Implement authentication and authorization, for example, using JWT (JSON Web Tokens) for user validation. For GraphQL, be mindful of querying patterns to prevent exposure of sensitive data.

4. Error Handling

Proper error handling enhances API usability. Design consistent error responses, whether it's a 404 Not Found in REST or a comprehensive GraphQL response structure.

5. Performance Monitoring

Utilize monitoring tools like Prometheus and Grafana, or application performance management tools like New Relic, to keep an eye on your APIs for performance metrics and error tracking.

In this chapter, we covered the fundamental aspects of creating and managing RESTful and GraphQL APIs with TypeScript. Both styles of APIs have their own use cases and best practices, and TypeScript helps ensure our code is more robust and maintainable. As you continue designing your APIs, remember to prioritize good documentation, versioning, security, and error handling for a successful API service.

Automating API Gateway and Load Balancer Configurations

In this chapter, we will explore how to automate the configurations of both API Gateways and Load Balancers using TypeScript, a language that offers type safety and modern programming paradigms often lacking in

JavaScript.

1. Understanding API Gateways and Load Balancers
1.1 API Gateway

An API Gateway acts as a single entry point for managing client requests to multiple backend services. It provides essential features such as:

Routing: Directing requests to appropriate services based on the incoming request.

Authentication and Authorization: Ensuring that only authorized requests are processed.

Rate Limiting: Protecting backend services from being overwhelmed by too many requests.

Caching: Improving performance by storing frequently requested data. ### 1.2 Load Balancer

A Load Balancer distributes incoming network traffic across multiple servers. Its objectives are to:

Ensure High Availability: Prevent any single server from becoming a point of failure.

Optimize Resource Use: Make the most efficient use of available resources.

Minimize Response Times: Enhance user experience by reducing the time it takes to respond to requests.

2. Setting Up the Environment ### 2.1 Prerequisites

Before diving into automation, ensure you have the following:

Node.js installed on your machine.

An understanding of TypeScript basics.

Access to cloud platforms like AWS, Google Cloud, or Azure, which provide API Gateways and Load Balancer services.

Familiarity with Infrastructure as Code (IaC) tools like Terraform or AWS CloudFormation, as they can be integrated with TypeScript for automation.

2.2 Project Initialization

Start by creating a new TypeScript project:

```bash
mkdir api-automation cd api-automation npm init -y
npm install typescript ts-node @types/node --save-dev


npx tsc --init
```

This initializes a new TypeScript project where we'll write our automation scripts. ## 3. Automation Design

For this example, we will use the AWS SDK for JavaScript to automate configurations for AWS API Gateway and Elastic Load Balancer (ELB). You can install the necessary packages using npm:

```bash
npm install @aws-sdk/client-api-gateway @aws-sdk/client-elastic-load-balancing
```

3.1 AWS API Gateway Automation

To automate API Gateway configurations, you need to

create a new API, define resources, and set up methods.

Here's a sample code snippet to create an API Gateway:

```typescript
```typescript import {
ApiGatewayManagementApiClient,
CreateRestApiCommand
} from "@aws-sdk/client-api-gateway";
const createApiGateway = async () => {
const client = new ApiGatewayManagementApiClient({
region: 'us-west-2' });

const command = new CreateRestApiCommand({ name:
"MyAPI",
description: "API for my application",
endpointConfiguration: {
types: ["REGIONAL"]
},
});
try {
const data = await client.send(command);
console.log("API Gateway created with ID:", data.id);
} catch (error) {
console.error("Error creating API Gateway:", error);
}
};
createApiGateway();
```
```

```
```

3.2 AWS Load Balancer Automation

Next, let's automate the creation of a Load Balancer. The following code snippet demonstrates how to create an Application Load Balancer (ALB):

```typescript
import {
ElasticLoadBalancingClient,
CreateLoadBalancerCommand
} from "@aws-sdk/client-elastic-load-balancing";

const createLoadBalancer = async () => {
const client = new ElasticLoadBalancingClient({ region: 'us-west-2' });

const command =
new CreateLoadBalancerCommand({ Name: "MyLoadBalancer",
Subnets: ["subnet-12345"], // replace with valid subnet IDs SecurityGroups: ["sg-12345"], // replace with valid security group IDs Scheme: "internet-facing",
Tags: [{
Key: "Name",
Value: "MyLoadBalancer"
}],
// More configurations can be added as needed
```

```
});
try {
const data = await client.send(command);
console.log("Load    Balancer    created    with    ARN:",
data.LoadBalancers?.[0].LoadBalancerArn);
} catch (error) {
console.error("Error creating Load Balancer:", error);
}
};
createLoadBalancer();
```
```

## 4. Handling Deployment

While the examples above will help you set up configurations, you'll likely want these processes to be embedded within a larger deployment pipeline. Here are some best practices for integrating these scripts:

**CI/CD Integration**: Use tools like Jenkins, GitHub Actions, or AWS CodePipeline to run these scripts automatically when code is merged into your main branch.

**Error Handling and Logging**: Implement proper error-handling mechanisms and logging to track issues during execution.

**Parameterization**: Create configurations outside the hardcoded values, perhaps utilizing environment variables or a configuration management tool.
```

Understanding and implementing these automation scripts can help streamline your workflow, reduce manual configuration overhead, and minimize human error. As cloud infrastructures evolve, leveraging modern programming languages like TypeScript for these tasks will become more critical to maintaining efficient and organized architecture.

Chapter 8: Managing Docker and Kubernetes with TypeScript

This chapter explores how TypeScript—an increasingly popular programming language known for its type safety and developer-friendly features—can be effectively utilized to manage Docker and Kubernetes environments.

8.1 Introduction to Docker and Kubernetes

Before delving into the specifics of using TypeScript with Docker and Kubernetes, it is essential to understand the fundamental concepts of these technologies.

8.1.1 Docker

Docker is a platform that enables developers to automate the deployment of applications within lightweight, portable containers. Each container encompasses the application and all its dependencies, ensuring consistent environments from development to production. Key benefits of Docker include:

Isolation: Each application runs in its container, minimizing conflicts.

Scalability: Containers can be easily replicated across multiple environments.

Portability: Docker containers can run on any system that has the Docker engine. ### 8.1.2 Kubernetes

Kubernetes (often abbreviated as K8s) is an open-source orchestration platform that automates the deployment, scaling, and management of containerized applications. It offers robust features for managing container lifecycles, including:

133

Load balancing: Distributing network traffic evenly across container instances.

Service discovery: Automatically locating and connecting services within the cluster.

Self-healing: Automatically replacing failed containers and ensuring application availability. ## 8.2 Setting Up Your TypeScript Project

To begin managing Docker and Kubernetes with TypeScript, you first need to set up a new TypeScript project. Here's a step-by-step guide to get started:

8.2.1 Initializing a TypeScript Project

Install Node.js: Ensure you have Node.js and npm (Node Package Manager) installed on your machine.

Initialize the Project: Create a new directory for your project and navigate to it in your terminal.

```bash
mkdir docker-k8s-typescript && cd docker-k8s-typescript
npm init -y
```

Install TypeScript:

```bash
npm install typescript --save-dev
```

Create a tsconfig.json:

```bash
npx tsc --init
```

```
```

This config file will allow you to customize your TypeScript compilation settings. ### 8.2.2 Installing Required Packages

You will need some additional packages to interact with Docker and Kubernetes from your TypeScript application. Install the following:

```bash
npm install axios dockerode @kubernetes/client-node @types/express express
```

`axios`: To make HTTP requests to the Docker and Kubernetes APIs.

`dockerode`: A Docker client for Node.js that allows you to manage Docker containers programmatically.

`@kubernetes/client-node`: A client library for interacting with Kubernetes clusters. ## 8.3 Managing Docker with TypeScript

In this section, we'll cover how to manage Docker containers using TypeScript. ### 8.3.1 Connecting to Docker

Create a new TypeScript file called `dockerManager.ts`, which will handle Docker operations. Start by importing the necessary modules and creating a Docker client instance:

```typescript
import Docker from 'dockerode';
```

```typescript
const docker = new Docker();
```

8.3.2 Creating and Starting Containers

To create and start a Docker container, you can define a function that will take parameters like the image name and configuration:

```typescript
async function createAndStartContainer(image: string) {
try {
const container = await docker.createContainer({ Image: image,
Tty: true,
});
await container.start();
console.log(`Container ${container.id} started.`);
} catch (error) {

console.error('Error starting container: ', error);
}
}
// Example usage createAndStartContainer('nginx:latest');
```

8.3.3 Stopping and Removing Containers

You can also implement functions to stop and remove containers:

```typescript
async function stopContainer(containerId: string) { const
container = docker.getContainer(containerId); await
container.stop();

console.log(`Container ${containerId} stopped.`);

}

async function removeContainer(containerId: string) {
const container = docker.getContainer(containerId);
await container.remove();

console.log(`Container ${containerId} removed.`);

}
```

8.4 Managing Kubernetes with TypeScript

Next, we will explore how to deploy and manage
applications on Kubernetes using TypeScript. ### 8.4.1
Connecting to Kubernetes

Create another TypeScript file called `k8sManager.ts`. To
interact with a Kubernetes cluster, initialize the
Kubernetes client:

```typescript
import * as k8s from '@kubernetes/client-node';

const kc = new k8s.KubeConfig();

kc.loadFromDefault(); // Load config from default
location

const k8sApi = kc.makeApiClient(k8s.CoreV1Api);
```

8.4.2 Managing Kubernetes Pods

You can create functions to list, create, and delete pods in a Kubernetes namespace:

```typescript
async function listPods(namespace: string) {

const res = await k8sApi.listNamespacedPod(namespace);
console.log('Pods:', res.body.items);

}


async function createPod(namespace: string, podManifest: k8s.V1Pod) { const res = await k8sApi.createNamespacedPod(namespace, podManifest); console.log(`Pod ${res.body.metadata?.name} created.`);

}
```

8.4.3 Deleting a Pod

To delete a specific pod, you can add the following function:

```typescript
async function deletePod(namespace: string, podName: string) { await k8sApi.deleteNamespacedPod(podName, namespace); console.log(`Pod ${podName} deleted.`);

}
```

8.5 Combining Docker and Kubernetes Management

By now, you have the basic building blocks to manage

138

Docker containers and Kubernetes pods. You can even create a higher-level manager that utilizes both Docker and Kubernetes functionalities:

8.5.1 Unified Manager Module

Create a new TypeScript file called `manager.ts` where you will import both `dockerManager` and

`k8sManager` modules, allowing centralized management of both technologies.

```typescript
import { createAndStartContainer, stopContainer, removeContainer } from './dockerManager'; import { listPods, createPod, deletePod } from './k8sManager';

// Example usage (async () => {

await createAndStartContainer('nginx:latest'); await listPods('default');

})();
```

We explored how to manage Docker and Kubernetes using TypeScript. By leveraging TypeScript's powerful typing system and modern development practices, you can create reliable and maintainable scripts for managing containerized applications and orchestration with Kubernetes.

Writing TypeScript Scripts to Automate Docker Builds and Containers

In contemporary software development, automation is the key to enhancing productivity and maintaining consistency. Docker, a popular platform for developing, shipping, and running applications in containers, lends itself well to automation scenarios. In this chapter, we will explore how to harness the power of TypeScript to automate Docker builds and manage containers, creating a seamless workflow that can improve collaborative development, testing, and deployment processes.

1. Understanding the Basics of Docker

Before diving into the automation scripts, it's essential to understand some fundamental concepts related to Docker:

Images: A Docker image is a blueprint for creating containers. It contains the executable code, libraries, dependencies, and other files needed to run an application.

Containers: A container is a lightweight, standalone unit that acts like a miniature virtual machine. It encapsulates the application and all of its dependencies, ensuring it runs consistently across different environments.

Dockerfile: This is a text file that contains instructions on how to build a Docker image. It defines the base image, libraries, and configurations necessary for your application.

2. Setting Up Your Environment

To automate Docker processes with TypeScript, you'll

need a few prerequisites:

Node.js and npm: Ensure you have Node.js installed. This will also install npm (Node Package Manager), which we'll use to manage our project dependencies.

TypeScript: Install TypeScript globally if you haven't already:

```bash
npm install -g typescript
```

Docker: Install Docker on your machine and ensure it's running. ## 3. Creating Your TypeScript Project

Let's set up a simple TypeScript project for our automation scripts.

Initialize a new Node.js project:

```bash
mkdir docker-automation cd docker-automation npm init -y
```

Install TypeScript and Dockerode: Dockerode is a Docker client for Node.js that allows us to interact with Docker APIs.

```bash
npm install typescript @types/node dockerode
```

Set up TypeScript configuration:

Create a `tsconfig.json` file to configure TypeScript:

```json
{

"compilerOptions": { "target": "es6", "module":
"commonjs", "outDir": "./dist", "strict": true

},

"include": ["src/**/*"]

}
```

Create your project structure:

```bash
mkdir src
```

4. Writing TypeScript Scripts ### 4.1 Creating a Docker Image

Let's start by creating a TypeScript script to build a Docker image from a Dockerfile.

Create a Dockerfile in the project root:

```dockerfile
FROM node:14

WORKDIR /usr/src/app COPY package*.json ./ RUN npm install COPY . .

CMD ["node", "index.js"]
```

Create a script to build the image:

Create a file named `buildImage.ts` in the `src` folder:

```typescript
import Docker from 'dockerode';
const docker = new Docker(); async function buildImage()
{
const dockerfilePath = './Dockerfile';
try {
const stream = await docker.buildImage(dockerfilePath, {
t: 'my-node-app' }); stream.on('data', (data) => {
console.log(data.toString());
});
stream.on('end', () => { console.log('Image built
successfully!');
});
stream.on('error', (error) => {
console.error('Error building the image:', error);
});
} catch (error) {
console.error('Failed to build image:', error);
}
}
buildImage();
```

4.2 Running a Docker Container

Next, let's create a script to run a Docker container using

the image we just built.

Create a script named `runContainer.ts` in the `src` folder:

```typescript
import Docker from 'dockerode';
const docker = new Docker(); async function runContainer(){
try {
const container = await docker.createContainer({ Image: 'my-node-app',
name: 'my_running_container', Tty: true,
ExposedPorts: { '3000/tcp': {}
},
HostConfig: { PortBindings: {
'3000/tcp': [{ HostPort: '3000'}]
}
}
});
await container.start();
console.log('Container started successfully: my_running_container');
} catch (error) {
console.error('Failed to run container:', error);
}
```

```
}
runContainer();
```

5. Combining the Scripts

To streamline your workflow, you can create a master script that builds the image and then runs the container automatically.

Create a file named `index.ts` in the `src` folder that combines both operations:

```typescript
import { buildImage } from './buildImage'; import { runContainer } from './runContainer';

async function main() { await buildImage(); await runContainer();
}
main();
```

Update the export statement in `buildImage.ts`: Ensure you export the `buildImage` function:

```typescript
export async function buildImage() {
// ... existing code
}
```

Update the export statement in `runContainer.ts`:

Similarly, export the `runContainer` function:

```typescript
export async function runContainer() {
// ... existing code
}
```

6. Running Your Scripts

Now that everything is set up, you can compile and run your automation scripts:

Compile the TypeScript code:

```bash npx tsc
```

Run the master script:

```bash
node dist/index.js
```

By writing scripts that utilize the Dockerode client, we're able to build images, create, and run containers efficiently. This approach not only simplifies repetitive tasks but also helps maintain a high level of consistency in your development and deployment processes.

Deploying and Managing Kubernetes Clusters with TypeScript

TypeScript, a superset of JavaScript, enhances code quality through static typing, thus allowing developers to catch errors at compile time. In this chapter, we will explore how to use TypeScript to deploy and manage Kubernetes clusters in a robust and efficient manner.

Setting the Stage: Prerequisites

Before diving into the technical aspects, you'll need a few prerequisites:

Node.js and npm: Ensure that you have the latest version of Node.js installed on your machine. npm (Node Package Manager) comes bundled with Node.js.

Kubernetes Cluster: Either set up your own Kubernetes cluster using tools like Minikube or use a managed service such as Google Kubernetes Engine (GKE) or Amazon EKS.

TypeScript: Ensure TypeScript is installed globally on your system. You can install it using npm:

```bash
npm install -g typescript
```

kubectl: The Kubernetes command-line tool, which interacts with your cluster. ## Setting Up Your TypeScript Project

Initialize the Project: Start by creating a new directory for your TypeScript project and navigate into it.

```bash
mkdir k8s-typescript cd k8s-typescript
```

Initialize npm: Run the following command to create a `package.json` file:

```bash npm init -y
```

Install Dependencies: You'll need some essential packages, such as TypeScript, and Kubernetes client libraries. For this example, we will use `@kubernetes/client-node`:

```bash
npm install @kubernetes/client-node typescript ts-node
```

Configure TypeScript: Create a `tsconfig.json` file to configure TypeScript settings:

```json
{
"compilerOptions": { "target": "es6", "module": "commonjs",

"strict": true, "esModuleInterop": true, "skipLibCheck": true,
"forceConsistentCasingInFileNames": true
```

```
}
}
```

Writing Code to Deploy a Kubernetes Pod

With the project set up, you can now write TypeScript code to deploy a Kubernetes pod.

Create a file named `deployPod.ts`:

```typescript
import * as k8s from '@kubernetes/client-node';

async function main() {

const kc = new k8s.KubeConfig(); kc.loadFromDefault();

const k8sApi = kc.makeApiClient(k8s.CoreV1Api); const podManifest = {

apiVersion: 'v1',

kind: 'Pod', metadata: {

name: 'my-pod', labels: {

app: 'my-app',

},

},

spec: {

containers: [

{

name: 'my-container', image: 'nginx:latest',

ports: [{ containerPort: 80 }],
```
149

```
    },
  ],
  },
};
try {
  const response = await
k8sApi.createNamespacedPod('default', podManifest);
  console.log('Pod created:',
response.body.metadata.name);
} catch (error) {
  console.error('Error creating pod:', error.body);
}
}
main();
```

Execute the Script: Run the script using `ts-node`:

```bash
npx ts-node deployPod.ts
```

Managing Kubernetes Resources

Managing Kubernetes resources such as deployments, services, and ConfigMaps can also be done with TypeScript. Below, we implement a simple example of creating a Deployment.

Create a file named `deployApp.ts`:

```typescript
import * as k8s from '@kubernetes/client-node';
async function main() {
const kc = new k8s.KubeConfig(); kc.loadFromDefault();
const k8sApi = kc.makeApiClient(k8s.AppsV1Api); const deploymentManifest = {
apiVersion: 'apps/v1',
kind: 'Deployment', metadata: {
name: 'my-deployment',
},
spec: {
replicas: 2, selector: {
matchLabels: { app: 'my-app',
},
},
template: { metadata: {
labels: {
app: 'my-app',
},
},
spec: {
containers: [
```

```
{
name: 'my-container', image: 'nginx:latest',
ports: [{ containerPort: 80 }],
},
],
},
},
},
};
try {
const          response          =          await
k8sApi.createNamespacedDeployment('default',
deploymentManifest); console.log('Deployment created:',
response.body.metadata.name);
} catch (error) {
console.error('Error creating deployment:', error.body);
}
}
main();
```

Execute the Script: As with the previous example, execute the script using:
```bash
npx ts-node deployApp.ts
```

```
```

Interacting with the Kubernetes API

In this chapter, you've learned to deploy a pod and a deployment to a Kubernetes cluster using TypeScript. You can further extend your application to interact with the Kubernetes API for various tasks, such as scaling deployments, deleting resources, and querying the status of resources.

The key takeaway from this chapter is that using TypeScript with the Kubernetes client library allows for better maintainability, improved error handling, and a robust development experience due to static typing. This approach can be seamlessly integrated into CI/CD pipelines, enabling automated deployments and management of Kubernetes resources.

As you deploy and manage Kubernetes clusters using TypeScript, remember to leverage the power of TypeScript's strong type system to catch potential issues early in the development process. The combination of Kubernetes and TypeScript brings a modern approach to cloud-native application development, ensuring that your infrastructure is not only scalable but also maintainable and error-resistant.

Chapter 9: Event-Driven Automation with TypeScript

This chapter delves into the concept of event-driven automation using TypeScript, a powerful superset of JavaScript that enhances development capabilities with static typing and modern features.

We will explore how to leverage TypeScript to create event-driven systems that automate workflows, respond to user actions, and integrate with various events from APIs and user interfaces. By the end of this chapter, you will understand how to design, implement, and optimize event-driven automation patterns in TypeScript.

1. Understanding Event-Driven Architecture

Before diving into implementation, it's essential to grasp the fundamentals of event-driven architecture. At its core, EDA is centered around events – signals that something has occurred within a system. These events can originate from user actions, system processes, or external APIs. The key components of an event-driven system include:

Event Producers: Entities that generate events. These can be user interactions, APIs, or other systems.

Event Consumers: Components that listen for and react to events. They execute specific actions in response.

Event Channels: Communication pathways through which events are transmitted between producers and consumers. These can be message queues, web sockets, or even direct function calls.

Benefits of Event-Driven Architecture

Decoupling: Event producers and consumers are loosely coupled, allowing changes in one without impacting the other.

Scalability: Systems can scale independently based on the event load, enabling more efficient resource utilization.

Responsiveness: Applications can react in real-time to incoming events, improving user experience. ## 2. Setting Up Your TypeScript Environment

To build an event-driven automation system, you need a properly configured TypeScript environment. Follow these steps to get started:

Install Node.js and TypeScript:

Make sure you have Node.js installed. Then you can use npm (Node Package Manager) to install TypeScript:

```bash
npm install -g typescript
```

Create a New Project:

Initialize a new directory for your TypeScript project:

```bash
mkdir event-driven-automation cd event-driven-automation npm init -y
```

```
```

Add TypeScript Configuration:

Create a `tsconfig.json` file to configure TypeScript:

```json
{
"compilerOptions": { "target": "ES6", "module": "commonjs", "outDir": "./dist", "strict": true
},
"include": ["src/**/*"], "exclude": ["node_modules"]
}
```

Create the Directory Structure:

Organize your project into `src` and `dist` folders:

```bash mkdir src mkdir dist
```

3. Implementing Event Producers

Event producers trigger events within your application. Let's create a simple example of a button click event using TypeScript:

3.1 DOM Event Producer

In `src/eventProducer.ts`, you can set up a button that generates an event when clicked:

```typescript
const button = document.createElement('button');
button.textContent = 'Click Me';
```

```
document.body.appendChild(button);

button.addEventListener('click', () => {

const event = new CustomEvent('myCustomEvent', {
detail: { message: 'Button clicked!' } });
window.dispatchEvent(event);

console.log('Event produced: ', event.detail.message);

});
```
```

### 3.2 Simulated API Event Producer

For server-side or simulated API events, you can use Node.js to generate events:

```typescript
import { EventEmitter } from 'events';

const apiEventEmitter = new EventEmitter();

function simulateApiEvent() { setInterval(() => {

apiEventEmitter.emit('dataReceived', { data: 'New data from API!' });

}, 5000);

}

simulateApiEvent();
```

4. Creating Event Consumers

Event consumers listen for the events produced and perform actions based on those events. In this section, you will create two types of consumers: one for the DOM

157
```

events and one for the API events.

4.1 DOM Event Consumer

In the same file, listen for the custom event generated by the button click:

```typescript
window.addEventListener('myCustomEvent', (event: CustomEvent) => { console.log('Event consumed: ', event.detail.message);
});
```

4.2 API Event Consumer

For the API event, you'll set up a listener that processes incoming data:

```typescript
apiEventEmitter.on('dataReceived', (data) => {

console.log('API event consumed: ', data.data);
});
```

5. Putting It All Together

Now that we have set up both producers and consumers, let's organize everything in a single file called `src/index.ts` and initiate the event-driven automation:

```typescript
// Import the producers and consumers import './eventProducer';
```

```
console.log('Event-driven automation is running...');
```

Compile the TypeScript files and serve them using a simple server or open `index.html` in the browser to see your event-driven automation framework in action.

6. Advancing with Event Buses

As systems grow, managing multiple event producers and consumers can become complex. Event buses offer a solution, acting as a central hub for event communication. You can create a simple event bus in TypeScript:

```typescript
class EventBus {

private listeners: { [event: string]: Function[] } = {};

on(event: string, listener: Function) { if (!this.listeners[event]) {

this.listeners[event] = [];

}

this.listeners[event].push(listener);

}

emit(event: string, data: any) { if (this.listeners[event]) {

this.listeners[event].forEach(listener => listener(data));

}

}

}

const eventBus = new EventBus();
```

6.1 Using the Event Bus

You can now modify your producers and consumers to use the event bus for better organization:

```typescript
eventBus.on('buttonClicked', (data) => {

console.log('Button event consumed: ', data.message);

});

// Emit the event from the button click
eventBus.emit('buttonClicked', { message: 'Button clicked!' });

```

We learned how to create event producers and consumers and explored the benefits of using an event bus to manage complex interactions within the system.

As you continue to build and scale your applications, consider how event-driven patterns can streamline automation and improve responsiveness. With TypeScript's type safety and modern features, your event-driven systems can become even more powerful and maintainable.

Using TypeScript for Webhooks and Event-Driven Architecture

One of the most practical applications of this paradigm is through webhooks, which are user-defined HTTP callbacks. In this chapter, we will explore how to effectively use TypeScript to implement webhooks and leverage event-driven architecture within your applications.

Understanding Webhooks

Webhooks provide a way for one application to send real-time data to another whenever a specific event occurs. For instance, if you are integrating with a payment gateway, you might set up a webhook to be notified every time a transaction is completed. This allows your application to react to the event without needing to poll the payment gateway regularly.

A Basic Example of a Webhook

Let's say we want to set up a webhook that listens for updates from a third-party service. We will create an Express.js application that receives and handles these updates. Here's a basic implementation in TypeScript:

```typescript
import express, { Request, Response } from 'express';

const app = express();

const PORT = process.env.PORT || 3000;

// Middleware to parse JSON payloads
app.use(express.json());

// Webhook endpoint

app.post('/webhook', (req: Request, res: Response) => {
const event = req.body;

// Process the event console.log('Received event: ', event);

// You can trigger further actions based on the event
switch (event.type) {
```

```
case 'payment_completed':
// Handle completed payment break;
case 'payment_failed':
// Handle failed payment break;
default:
console.warn('Unknown event type:', event.type);
}

res.sendStatus(200); // Respond to acknowledge receipt
of the event
});


// Start the server app.listen(PORT, () => {
console.log(`Server           is          running        on
http://localhost:${PORT}`);
});
```
```

### Webhook Security

When implementing webhooks, security should be a top priority. Webhooks can be susceptible to spoofing, where an attacker sends fake requests to your application. Here are a few strategies to enhance webhook security in your TypeScript applications:

**Secret Token Verification**: Most services provide a method to include a secret token in the request headers. Verify this token in your webhook handler.

**IP Whitelisting**: If possible, restrict incoming requests
```

to known IP addresses.

Rate Limiting: Implement rate limiting to prevent abuse from malicious actors.

Response Codes: Always send appropriate HTTP status codes. A 2xx status indicates your application received the event successfully.

Event-Driven Architecture with TypeScript

An event-driven architecture allows different components of your application to communicate through events, decoupling their interactions. TypeScript's static typing offers clear benefits in building such architecture, making your implementation more manageable and robust.

Setting Up an Event Emitter

In Node.js, you can use the built-in `EventEmitter` class to create an event-driven structure. Here's how to set up a basic event emitter using TypeScript:

```typescript
import { EventEmitter } from 'events';

// Create an instance of EventEmitter const eventEmitter = new EventEmitter();

// Define event handler eventEmitter.on('user_registered', (userData) => {

console.log(`User registered: ${JSON.stringify(userData)}`);

});

// Trigger the event when a user registers

const registerUser = (userData: { name: string; email:
```

```
string }) => {
```

// Simulate saving user to the database
console.log('Saving user to the database...');

// Emit user_registration event
eventEmitter.emit('user_registered', userData);

```
};
```

// Register a new user

registerUser({ name: 'John Doe', email: 'john.doe@example.com' });

` ` `

Integrating Webhooks and Events

By integrating webhooks with event-driven architecture, you can build a responsive system that reacts to real-time events. This promotes a clear flow of data and minimizes the coupling between components.

Here's how you might do that:

Webhook Receives Event: Your webhook receives data from a third-party service and parses it.

Emitting Events: Based on the parsed data, you emit events that trigger various handlers in your application.

Listening for Events: Other components of your application listen for these events and take appropriate actions.

Example Integration

Let's combine our earlier webhook example with the event

emitter:

```typescript
app.post('/webhook', (req: Request, res: Response) => {
const event = req.body;
```

console.log('Received event: ', event);

```
// Emit events based on webhook data switch (event.type)
{
```

case   'payment_completed':
eventEmitter.emit('payment_completed',   event.data);
break;

case   'payment_failed':
eventEmitter.emit('payment_failed',event.data); break;

default:

console.warn('Unknown event type:', event.type);

}

res.sendStatus(200);

});

//   Additional   event   listeners
eventEmitter.on('payment_completed',(data)=> {

console.log('Processing payment completion for:', data);

// Implement business logic for completed payments

});

eventEmitter.on('payment_failed',   (data)   =>   {
console.log('Handling payment failure for:', data);

```
// Implement business logic for failed payments
});
```

Best Practices

Use Strong Typing: Define interfaces for your events and webhook payloads to ensure validity. This promotes better code clarity and reduces bugs.

```typescript
interface PaymentEvent {
type: 'payment_completed' | 'payment_failed'; data: {
amount: number; currency: string; transactionId: string;
};
}
```

Decoupling: Keep your Webhook handling logic separate from business logic. This makes it easier to maintain and extend.

Testing: Use unit tests and integration tests to ensure your webhook handling and event emissions work as expected.

Logging: Implement structured logging for all webhook events. This aids in tracking issues and understanding application behavior in production.

By leveraging strong typing, clear architecture, and effective security practices, you can create robust systems

166

that handle real-time events with minimal friction. In the ensuing complexity of modern web applications, mastering these concepts will prepare you to build scalable and reliable solutions.

Building Serverless Functions with TypeScript for DevOps

This chapter delves into building serverless functions using TypeScript, a language that brings type safety and modern syntax enhancements to JavaScript. As we combine serverless computing with DevOps principles, we empower teams to deliver code quickly and effectively while maintaining high levels of reliability and performance.

1. Understanding Serverless Computing

Before diving into the implementation, it's important to grasp what serverless computing actually entails. Contrary to its name, serverless does not eliminate servers; rather, it abstracts much of the server management away from the developer. In a serverless model, the cloud provider handles server provisioning, scaling, and maintenance, allowing developers to focus solely on writing and deploying code.

Benefits of Serverless Architecture

Cost Efficiency: Pay-as-you-go pricing models mean you only pay for the compute resources you consume.

Scalability: Automatic scaling allows functions to handle varying loads seamlessly.

Reduced Operational Complexity: Developers can

deploy and manage applications without worrying about underlying infrastructure.

2. The Role of TypeScript

TypeScript enhances JavaScript by providing static typing, interfaces, and advanced tooling capabilities, making it particularly suited for developing serverless functions. With TypeScript, developers can catch errors at compile time, improving code quality and maintainability.

Why TypeScript for Serverless Functions?

Type Safety: Avoid common pitfalls associated with dynamic typing in JavaScript.

Enhanced Development Experience: Features such as autocompletion and inline documentation improve productivity.

Seamless Adoption: TypeScript can easily interoperate with existing JavaScript code, facilitating transition and integration.

3. Setting Up the Environment

To begin building serverless functions with TypeScript, the following tools and services are commonly used:

Node.js: The runtime environment for executing TypeScript.

Serverless Framework: A tool that simplifies the deployment and management of serverless applications.

AWS Lambda or **Azure Functions**: The cloud providers offering serverless function performability.

Installation

Install Node.js from the official website.

Set up the Serverless Framework globally:

```bash
npm install -g serverless
```

Initialize a new Serverless project:

```bash
serverless create --template aws-nodejs-typescript --path
my-serverless-app cd my-serverless-app
```

Install TypeScript and the required dependencies:

```bash
npm install --save-dev typescript ts-node @types/node
```

4. Writing Your First Serverless Function

Let's walk through the creation of a simple serverless function that responds to HTTP requests. ### Step 1: Configure `serverless.yml`

The `serverless.yml` file is the backbone of your serverless application. It defines the cloud provider, service configuration, and the functions to deploy. Here's a sample configuration:

```yaml
service: my-serverless-app
```

```yaml
provider:
name: aws
runtime: nodejs14.x
functions:
hello:
handler: handler.hello events:
- http:
path: hello method: get
```

Step 2: Write the Function

Open the `handler.ts` file and add the following code:

```typescript
import { APIGatewayEvent, Context, Callback } from 'aws-lambda';

export const hello = async (event: APIGatewayEvent, context: Context, callback: Callback) => { const response = {
statusCode: 200,
body: JSON.stringify({
message: 'Hello, Serverless with TypeScript!',
}),

};
return response;
```

```
};
```

Step 3: Deploy the Function

Deploy the function to the cloud provider:

```bash
serverless deploy
```

Once the deployment is complete, you'll receive an endpoint URL to trigger your function. Use a tool like Postman or curl to send a GET request to this URL, and you should see the desired response.

5. Testing and Debugging

Testing serverless functions developed in TypeScript can be achieved through various means:

Unit Testing: Leverage testing frameworks like Jest or Mocha to create unit tests for your functions.

Local Development: Use the Serverless Offline plugin for running your functions locally, allowing you to debug and test as if they were in production.

Configuring Jest might look like this:

```bash
npm install --save-dev jest ts-jest @types/jest
```

Then, create a test file (e.g., `handler.test.ts`) and write your tests. ## 6. Integrating with DevOps Practices

Serverless functions can easily fit into a DevOps workflow.

By automating deployments with CI/CD pipelines, you streamline the process of code integration and delivery. Tools like AWS CodePipeline or GitHub Actions can be leveraged to automate testing and deployment based on code commits.

Example CI/CD Pipeline with GitHub Actions

A sample GitHub Action file (`.github/workflows/deploy.yml`) can be set up for continuous deployment:

```yaml
name: Deploy Serverless

on:

push:

branches:

- main

jobs:

deploy:

runs-on: ubuntu-latest steps:

- uses: actions/checkout@v2
```

name: Set up Node.js

uses: actions/setup-node@v2 with:

node-version: '14'

run: npm install

```
run: npm run build
```

```
name: Deploy to AWS run: npx serverless deploy env:
AWS_ACCESS_KEY_ID:                          ${{
secrets.AWS_ACCESS_KEY_ID                      }}
AWS_SECRET_ACCESS_KEY:                       ${{
secrets.AWS_SECRET_ACCESS_KEY }}
```

7. Best Practices

To effectively harness the power of serverless architecture with TypeScript, consider the following best practices:

Keep Functions Small: Aim for single-responsibility functions that perform specific tasks.

Use Environment Variables: Store sensitive information securely by utilizing environment variables.

Monitor and Log: Implement logging and monitoring to capture insights about function performance and errors.

Optimize Cold Start: Be mindful of cold starts, especially for applications where response time is critical.

By abstracting away server management and leveraging rich tooling capabilities, teams can focus on delivering high-quality software rapidly and efficiently.

Chapter 10: Logging, Monitoring, and Alerting with TypeScript

Proper logging, monitoring, and alerting can make the difference between a smoothly running application and one that suffers from undiagnosed issues. In this chapter, we will explore how to effectively integrate logging and monitoring practices into your TypeScript applications.

Introduction to Logging

Logging is the practice of recording application events, errors, and other critical information to a log file or monitoring system. In TypeScript applications, the goal of logging is to provide valuable insights into system behavior, facilitate debugging, and help diagnose issues before they escalate.

Why Logging Matters

Debugging: Logs serve as a primary tool for developers to troubleshoot and resolve issues in real-time.

Auditing: Keeping track of events can provide a historical record of application behavior, which is essential for compliance and auditing purposes.

Performance Monitoring: Logs can be used to track application performance, such as response times and resource utilization, enabling teams to optimize efficiency.

Setting Up Logging in TypeScript

When it comes to logging in TypeScript, a structured logging approach can yield better results than a simple console log. One of the most popular libraries for logging in Node.js applications is `winston`, which is highly configurable and supports various transports (e.g., files, databases, external services).

Installing Winston

To install `winston`, use npm or yarn:

```bash
npm install winston
```

Basic Winston Configuration

Below is a simple example of setting up a basic logging system with Winston in a TypeScript project:

```typescript
import { createLogger, format, transports } from 'winston';
// Create a logger instance const logger = createLogger({
level: 'info',
format: format.combine( format.timestamp(),
format.json()
),


transports: [
new transports.Console(),
new transports.File({ filename: 'error.log', level: 'error' }),
new transports.File({ filename: 'combined.log' })
],
});
```

```
// Usage examples logger.info('This is an info log');
logger.error('This is an error log');
```

Log Levels

Winston supports several log levels out of the box:

`error`: Designates error events that might still allow the application to continue running.

`warn`: Represents potentially harmful situations.

`info`: Information messages that convey significant application flow.

`http`: Log HTTP requests/responses.

`verbose`: More detailed information than `info`, typically for debug purposes.

`debug`: Fine-grain messages for debugging purposes.

`silly`: Very detailed debug information.

By structuring your logs with these levels, you can filter and search through them more easily, making it simpler to pinpoint critical errors when needed.

Monitoring and Performance Metrics

While logging provides insight into specific events and errors, monitoring tools help you observe the overall health and performance of your application. They allow you to track metrics such as uptime, response time, and resource utilization.

Using Prometheus and Grafana

Prometheus is a powerful open-source monitoring system,

while Grafana is a visualization tool that can display metrics collected by Prometheus in visually appealing dashboards. Together, they make a robust solution for monitoring TypeScript applications.

Setting Up Prometheus

To add Prometheus monitoring to your TypeScript application, you can use an HTTP metrics library like `prom-client`. First, install it:

```bash
npm install prom-client
```

Next, set up a basic endpoint in your application that reports metrics:

```typescript
import express from 'express';
import { collectDefaultMetrics, register, Histogram, Counter } from 'prom-client';

const app = express(); const port = 3000;

// Collect default metrics collectDefaultMetrics();

// Create a custom metric
const httpRequestDurationMicroseconds = new Histogram({ name: 'http_request_duration_seconds',

help: 'Duration of HTTP requests in seconds', labelNames: ['method', 'route', 'code'],

});

// Middleware to measure request duration app.use((req,
```

```
res, next) => {

const                      end                      =
httpRequestDurationMicroseconds.startTimer();
res.on('finish', () => {

end({ method: req.method, route: req.originalUrl, code:
res.statusCode });

});

next();

});

// Expose metrics at /metrics endpoint app.get('/metrics',
async   (req,   res)   =>   {   res.set('Content-Type',
register.contentType); res.end(await register.metrics());

});

app.listen(port, () => {

console.log(`Server running on port ${port}`);

});

```
```

Visualizing Metrics with Grafana

To visualize the data collected by Prometheus, you can set
up Grafana. Create a new dashboard and add queries
based on the metrics you've implemented. With Grafana,
you can set up alerting rules that notify you if certain
thresholds are met, such as high latency or error rates.

Alerting Strategies

Alerts are essential for promptly addressing issues that
arise from your application. In a TypeScript project, you
```

can configure alerts based on logs and metrics using various tools.

Configuring Alerts in Grafana

Set Up Alerts: Go to your Grafana dashboard and create an alert based on a chosen metric.

Notification Channels: Set up notification channels such as email, Slack, or PagerDuty for your team to receive alerts.

Conditions: Define conditions for when alerts should trigger, such as when error rates exceed a certain level or when the application's response time surpasses a specific threshold.

By integrating alerting into your monitoring, you'll gain the ability to respond quickly to issues that could impact your users.

Best Practices for Logging, Monitoring, and Alerting

As you adopt logging, monitoring, and alerting in your TypeScript application, consider the following best practices:

Log Meaningful Information: Avoid cluttering logs with unnecessary details. Focus on logging significant events, such as errors, warnings, and critical application flows.

Use Structured Logging: Structured logs (JSON format, for instance) can simplify log parsing, allowing you to extract and analyze data more efficiently.

Centralized Logging: Utilize centralized logging solutions such as ELK (Elasticsearch, Logstash, Kibana) stack to aggregate logs from multiple services for seamless searching and monitoring.

Establish Alerting Thresholds: Define clear thresholds for alerting to minimize noise and ensure that alerts are actionable.

Regularly Review Logs and Metrics: Conduct regular reviews of your logging and monitoring practices to adapt to changing application needs and emerging issues.

We delved into setting up a logging system using Winston, collecting metrics with Prometheus, and visualizing and alerting with Grafana. By adhering to best practices and employing the proper tools, you can ensure that your applications are resilient, efficient, and responsive to issues as they arise. Embracing these practices will not only improve your application's reliability but also enhance the development and operational experience for your team.

Collecting and Analyzing Logs with TypeScript and Elastic Stack

This chapter will explore how to leverage TypeScript and the Elastic Stack (often referred to as the ELK Stack, which comprises Elasticsearch, Logstash, Kibana, and Beats) for robust log management. We will guide you through the process of collecting logs from a TypeScript application, sending them to the Elastic Stack, and harnessing Kibana for insightful analysis.

Understanding the Elastic Stack

The Elastic Stack provides a powerful set of tools for log management and analysis:

Elasticsearch: A distributed search and analytics engine that stores and indexes logs for fast retrieval.

Logstash: A data processing pipeline that ingests logs from various sources, transforms them, and stores them in Elasticsearch.

Kibana: A visualization tool that allows users to explore, visualize, and analyze data stored in Elasticsearch.

Beats: Lightweight data shippers that send data from various sources to Logstash or Elasticsearch directly.

Setting Up the Elastic Stack

To get started, you'll need to set up the Elastic Stack. This process involves installing Elasticsearch, Logstash, and Kibana. Follow the steps below:

Install Elasticsearch:

Download and install Elasticsearch from the official website.

Start the Elasticsearch service and verify it's running by navigating to `http://localhost:9200`.

Install Logstash:

Download and install Logstash.

Create a configuration file (e.g., `logstash.conf`) that

defines input, filter, and output plugins for processing logs.

Install Kibana:

Download and install Kibana.

Start the Kibana service and access it via `http://localhost:5601`. ## Collecting Logs in TypeScript

Once you have the Elastic Stack set up, the next step is to create a simple TypeScript application that generates logs.

Setting Up Your TypeScript Project:

```bash
mkdir ts-log-collector cd ts-log-collector npm init -y

npm install typescript ts-node winston npx tsc --init
```

The above commands create a new directory, initialize a Node.js project, install TypeScript, and set up the TypeScript configuration.

Logging with Winston:

Install the Winston library, a versatile logging library for Node.js.

```typescript
// src/logger.ts

import { createLogger, format, transports } from 'winston';

const logger = createLogger({ level: 'info',

format: format.combine( format.timestamp(), format.json()
```

```
),
transports: [
new transports.Console(),
new transports.File({ filename: 'logs/application.log' })
]
});
export default logger;
```

This simple logger writes logs to both the console and a file.

Integrating Logger in Your Application:

Create a sample application that uses this logger to generate logs of various levels.

```typescript
// src/app.ts
import logger from './logger';

const main = () => { logger.info('Application is starting...'); logger.warn('This is a warning message'); logger.error('An error occurred');
};

main();
```

Sending Logs to Logstash

To forward logs from your TypeScript application to Logstash, you can use a variety of methods, but one effective way is to use Filebeat.

Install Filebeat:

Download and install Filebeat from the Elastic website.

Configure Filebeat:

Update the Filebeat configuration file (e.g., `filebeat.yml`) to track the log files generated by your application.

```yaml
filebeat.inputs:

type: log paths:

- /path/to/your/project/logs/*.log

output.logstash:

hosts: ["localhost:5044"]
```

Make sure to adjust the path to point to your log file location.

Start Filebeat:

Run Filebeat to start sending logs to your Logstash instance. ## Configuring Logstash

Now, configure Logstash to handle the incoming logs from Filebeat.

Creating Logstash Pipeline:

Update your `logstash.conf` file to define the input from Filebeat, any required filters (e.g., parsing), and the output to Elasticsearch.

```plaintext
input {
```

```
beats {
port => 5044
}
}
filter {
# You can add filters here, like parsing JSON logs or
adding metadata
}
output {
elasticsearch {
hosts => ["http://localhost:9200"]
index => "application-logs-%{+YYYY.MM.dd}"
}
}
```

Starting Logstash:

Start Logstash with your configuration file in place.

```bash
bin/logstash -f logstash.conf
```

Analyzing Logs with Kibana

Once logs are flowing into Elasticsearch, you can use Kibana to visualize and analyze them.

Access Kibana:

Open your web browser and navigate to `http://localhost:5601`.

Creating an Index Pattern:

Go to the "Index Patterns" section and create a new index pattern matching the indices created by Logstash (e.g., `application-logs-*`).

Visualizing Logs:

Use Kibana's Discover feature to explore your logs. You can filter, sort, and search through the logs, creating visualizations to display trends or anomalies.

Creating Dashboards:

Assemble various visualizations into dashboards to keep track of the performance and health of your application.

This combined approach allows developers to gain deep insights into application behavior, troubleshoot issues effectively, and optimize performance. As systems grow and evolve, having a solid logging strategy is not just beneficial but essential for maintaining reliability and delivering quality software.

Setting Up Automated Alerts and Notifications with TypeScript

This chapter will guide you through setting up automated alerts and notifications using TypeScript, a powerful superset of JavaScript that brings type safety and better tooling to the development experience.

Understanding Alerts and Notifications

Before diving into implementation, it's essential to understand what alerts and notifications are. Alerts are immediate broadcasts meant to notify users or systems about significant events or changes, whereas notifications can be broader, encompassing reminders, updates, or promotional messages.

Use Cases for Alerts and Notifications

System Monitoring: Alerting developers or administrators when system metrics (CPU usage, memory, etc.) exceed specified thresholds.

User Activity: Notifying administrators about abnormal user behaviors, seen in applications like e-commerce sites.

Error Tracking: Sending alerts when exceptions or errors occur in an application.

Time-sensitive Reminders: Alerting users of upcoming deadlines or events. ## Setting Up the Environment

Before we start coding, ensure you have the following prerequisites:

Node.js: Ensure that Node.js is installed on your machine. This will allow you to run TypeScript and other JavaScript modules easily.

TypeScript: Install TypeScript globally with npm:

```bash
npm install -g typescript
```

Development Dependencies: Create a new project directory and initialize a new npm project:

```bash
mkdir automated-alerts cd automated-alerts npm init -y
```

Install TypeScript: After initializing the npm project, install TypeScript as a local dependency:

```bash
npm install typescript --save-dev
```

Initialize TypeScript: Create a new `tsconfig.json` file:

```bash
npx tsc --init
```

Building the Notification System ### Step 1: Create a Basic Alert Class

We will start by creating a basic Alert class. This class will serve as the foundation for our notifications.

```typescript
// src/alerts.ts export class Alert {

constructor(private message: string) {}

sendNotification() {

console.log(`Alert: ${this.message}`);

// Here, you could integrate email or SMS notification
```

188

services.

```
}
}
```

Step 2: Implementing Different Alert Types

Next, we can extend the `Alert` class to handle different types of notifications such as email or SMS.

```typescript
// src/alerts.ts

export class EmailAlert extends Alert {
constructor(private email: string, message: string) {

super(message);

}

sendNotification() {

console.log(`Sending email to ${this.email}: ${this.message}`);

// Integrate with an email service API here.

}
}

export class SMSAlert extends Alert {

constructor(private phoneNumber: string, message: string) { super(message);

}

sendNotification() {
```

```typescript
console.log(`Sending SMS to ${this.phoneNumber}:
${this.message}`);
// Integrate with an SMS service API here.
  }
}
```

Step 3: Triggering Alerts Automatically

Now that we have our alert types, we need a mechanism to trigger these alerts automatically based on specific conditions. For demonstration purposes, let's create a file that checks the CPU usage and sends alerts based on controlled thresholds.

```typescript
// src/systemMonitor.ts

import { EmailAlert, SMSAlert } from './alerts';

class SystemMonitor {

private cpuUsageThreshold: number;

constructor(threshold: number) { this.cpuUsageThreshold = threshold;
}

checkCpuUsage(cpuUsage: number) {

if (cpuUsage > this.cpuUsageThreshold) {

const emailAlert = new EmailAlert('admin@example.com', `CPU Usage Alert: ${cpuUsage}% exceeds the threshold of ${this.cpuUsageThreshold}%.`);
```

```
emailAlert.sendNotification();
const smsAlert = new SMSAlert('+1234567890', `CPU
Usage Alert: ${cpuUsage}% exceeds the threshold!`);
smsAlert.sendNotification();
}
}
}
// Simulating CPU usage checks every few seconds
const monitor = new SystemMonitor(75); // Threshold set
to 75% setInterval(() => {
const simulatedCpuUsage = Math.random() * 100; // Just
a    simulation    console.log(`Current    CPU    Usage:
${simulatedCpuUsage.toFixed(2)}%`);
monitor.checkCpuUsage(simulatedCpuUsage);
}, 3000);
```

Step 4: Running the Application

To execute your project, you need to compile your TypeScript code and then run the generated JavaScript files.

Compile the TypeScript files:

```bash
npx tsc
```

Run your application:

```bash
```

191

```
node dist/systemMonitor.js
```
```

We built a straightforward alert system capable of sending email and SMS notifications based on specific conditions, such as CPU usage. With this implementation, you can enhance your applications to be more responsive and user-friendly.

Moving forward, you can consider integrating with third-party services like SendGrid for email notifications or Twilio for SMS alerts to make your alert system even more robust and functional. Dedicate time to explore additional features, such as user-triggered alerts, customizable thresholds, and multi-channel notifications.
```

Chapter 11: Testing and Debugging DevOps Scripts in TypeScript

TypeScript, with its strong typing system and modern JavaScript features, provides an excellent choice for writing DevOps scripts that are both maintainable and scalable. In this chapter, we will explore effective methods for testing and debugging these scripts. We will cover various testing frameworks, debugging tools, and best practices for ensuring that your TypeScript DevOps scripts perform as intended.

1. Why Testing Matters

Testing is an essential component of any software development process, and DevOps is no exception. By ensuring that scripts are well-tested, we can:

Reduce Errors: Identify and fix bugs before they can cause issues in production.

Improve Reliability: Ensure that scripts behave consistently across different environments.

Enhance Maintainability: Facilitate changes and updates to scripts without introducing new bugs.

Documentation: Provide examples of expected behavior and usage. ## 2. Setting Up Your Testing Environment

Before we dive into writing tests, let's set up a typical TypeScript project that includes testing capabilities. We'll use [Jest](https://jestjs.io/) as our testing framework due to its popularity, ease of use, and comprehensive feature set.

2.1 Installing Dependencies

First, make sure you have Node.js and npm installed. Then, create a new project directory and install the necessary dependencies:

```bash
mkdir my-devops-scripts cd my-devops-scripts npm init -y

npm install typescript jest ts-jest @types/jest --save-dev
```

2.2 Configuring TypeScript and Jest

Next, create a `tsconfig.json` file to configure the TypeScript compiler:

```json
{
"compilerOptions": { "target": "ES6", "module": "CommonJS", "strict": true, "esModuleInterop": true
},
"include": ["src/**/*.ts"], "exclude": ["node_modules"]
}
```

Now, configure Jest by creating a `jest.config.js` file:

```javascript
module.exports = { preset: 'ts-jest', testEnvironment: 'node',
};
```

3. Writing Tests for TypeScript Scripts

With the setup complete, we can start writing tests for our TypeScript DevOps scripts. ### 3.1 Sample DevOps Script

Let's assume we have a simple script, `deploy.ts`, that simulates a deployment:

```typescript
// src/deploy.ts
export function deploy(app: string): string { if (!app) {
throw new Error('Application name cannot be empty');
}
return `Deploying ${app}...`;
}
```

3.2 Creating Test Cases

Next, we will create a test file, `deploy.test.ts`, to verify the behavior of our `deploy` function:

```typescript
// src/deploy.test.ts
import { deploy } from './deploy';
describe('deploy', () => {
test('should deploy the specified application', () => { const result = deploy('MyApp'); expect(result).toBe('Deploying MyApp...');
});
test('should throw an error when application name is
```

```
empty',          ()          =>          {          expect(()          =>
deploy('')).toThrow('Application name cannot be empty');
});
});
```

3.3 Running the Tests

To run the tests, simply use the following command in your terminal:

```bash
`` `bash npx jest
`` `
```

You should see output indicating that the tests have passed successfully. ## 4. Debugging TypeScript Scripts

Debugging is a critical skill for any developer. Setting up a workflow that allows for effective debugging of TypeScript DevOps scripts can significantly reduce development time and increase reliability.

4.1 Using Console Logging

The simplest form of debugging is using `console.log()` statements to output variable values or program states at various points in your code. For example:

```typescript
export function deploy(app: string): string {
console.log(`Attempting to deploy: ${app}`); if (!app) {

throw new Error('Application name cannot be empty');

}
```

```
return `Deploying ${app}...`;
}
```

4.2 Using a Debugger

TypeScript integrates well with popular IDEs like Visual Studio Code, which provides a built-in debugger. To set up debugging:

Open the `Run and Debug` panel in VS Code.

Create a new launch configuration by clicking on `create a launch.json file`.

Select Node.js, and a default configuration will be generated for you.

Here's a sample configuration:

```json
{
"version": "0.2.0", "configurations": [
{
"type": "node",
"request": "launch", "name": "Launch Program",
"program": "${workspaceFolder}/src/deploy.ts",
"preLaunchTask": "tsc: build - tsconfig.json", "outFiles":
["${workspaceFolder}/dist/**/*.js"]
}
]
}
```

```
` ` `
```

4.3 Debugging with Breakpoints

Insert breakpoints by clicking on the gutter next to the line numbers in your source code.

Start debugging using the `Run` button or by selecting the configuration you set up earlier. The debugger will pause at each breakpoint, allowing you to inspect variables and control flow.

5. Best Practices for Testing and Debugging

Alongside the techniques discussed, here are some best practices to follow for effective testing and debugging in TypeScript:

Write Tests First (TDD): Adopt a Test-Driven Development (TDD) approach to ensure your code is always covered by tests.

Use Meaningful Names: Give your tests meaningful names that indicate what behavior is being tested.

Continuous Integration: Integrate testing within your CI/CD pipeline to run tests automatically on commits.

Code Reviews: Conduct code reviews to catch potential issues before they become problematic.

Error Handling: Implement robust error handling in your scripts to provide meaningful feedback during failures.

By setting up a solid testing framework and utilizing effective debugging tools and techniques, you can create automation scripts that not only meet your operational needs but also allow for scalability and maintainability.

Unit Testing and Integration Testing for TypeScript DevOps Scripts

TypeScript, a superset of JavaScript, is increasingly gaining popularity due to its static typing and enhanced tooling capabilities. When developing DevOps scripts in TypeScript, it is essential to implement a robust testing strategy. This chapter delves into unit testing and integration testing, two critical components of a comprehensive testing framework that ensures the reliability of TypeScript DevOps scripts.

Understanding Unit Testing ### What is Unit Testing?

Unit testing involves writing tests for small, isolated pieces of code, typically individual functions or classes. The goal is to verify that each unit of code performs as expected. In the context of TypeScript DevOps scripts, unit tests can validate utilities, helpers, and core functionalities in isolation from the broader application.

Why Unit Test in TypeScript?

Catching Bugs Early: Unit tests help identify issues at an early stage, which is especially crucial in scripts that automate critical DevOps tasks.

Refactoring Confidence: With a solid suite of unit tests, developers can refactor code with confidence, knowing that any changes will be validated by existing tests.

Documentation: Well-written unit tests serve as additional documentation, providing examples of how functions are used and what inputs/outputs can be expected.

Tools for Unit Testing in TypeScript

Several tools can facilitate unit testing in TypeScript:

Jest: A popular testing framework that supports TypeScript out of the box. Jest provides an easy-to-use API and offers features like mocking, spies, and snapshot testing.

Mocha & Chai: A flexible testing framework (Mocha) combined with an assertion library (Chai) provides a customizable testing environment.

ts-jest: A Jest transformer that allows it to work with TypeScript files seamlessly, making it a go-to choice for TypeScript projects.

Writing Unit Tests

When writing unit tests for a TypeScript DevOps script, follow these best practices:

Isolate Tests: Ensure that each unit test only tests one specific functionality.

Use Mocks and Stubs: For functions that rely on external systems (like APIs or databases), use mocking libraries like Jest or Sinon to create mocks or stubs.

Test Edge Cases: Consider edge cases and potential failure scenarios to ensure that your functions handle unexpected inputs gracefully.

Here is a basic example of a unit test written in TypeScript using Jest:

```typescript
// util.ts - A simple utility function for parsing version strings

export function parseVersion(versionString: string): { major: number; minor: number; patch: number } { const parts = versionString.split('.').map(Number);

if (parts.length !== 3) {

throw new Error('Invalid version string format');

}

return { major: parts[0], minor: parts[1], patch: parts[2] };

}

// util.test.ts - Unit tests for the utility function import { parseVersion } from './util';

describe('parseVersion', () => {

it('should correctly parse valid version strings', () => { expect(parseVersion('1.0.0')).toEqual({ major: 1, minor: 0, patch: 0 });

});

it('should throw an error for invalid version strings', () => {

expect(() => parseVersion('1.0')).toThrow('Invalid version string format');

});

});
```

Understanding Integration Testing ### What is

Integration Testing?

Integration testing focuses on testing the interactions between components or systems when they are integrated together. In the realm of TypeScript DevOps scripts, this type of testing is crucial for verifying the correctness of interactions with external services, APIs, or configurations.

Importance of Integration Testing

Validate Interactions: Ensure that your scripts interact correctly with external systems, APIs, or databases.

Identify Issues Early: Integration tests help catch issues related to dependencies and interactions that may not be evident in unit tests.

End-to-End Confidence: It increases the confidence that your entire DevOps pipeline operates as intended, from triggering a build to deployment.

Tools for Integration Testing

Similar to unit testing, several tools can assist with integration testing in TypeScript:

Jest: Apart from unit testing, Jest can also be utilized for integration tests, especially with its built-in capabilities for handling async code.

Supertest: A library for testing HTTP servers in Node.js, useful for integration tests involving web APIs.

Cypress: Although primarily used for end-to-end testing, Cypress can also handle integration tests and is particularly powerful for web applications.

Writing Integration Tests

When conducting integration testing for TypeScript DevOps scripts, consider these best practices:

Use Realistic Test Environments: Mimic production environments where possible. Utilizing Docker containers for dependencies is a common practice.

Limit External Calls: With integration tests, aim to limit unnecessary calls to third-party services to maintain reliability and consistency.

Data Cleanup: Ensure that tests clean up any test data created to avoid polluting your data store.

Here is an example of an integration test using Jest and Supertest:

```typescript
// server.ts - A simple Express server import express from
'express';

const app = express(); app.get('/api/version', (req, res) =>
{
res.json({ version: '1.0.0' });
});

export default app;

// server.test.ts - Integration tests for the Express server
import request from 'supertest';

import app from './server';

describe('GET /api/version', () => {

it('should return a version object', async () => {
```

```
const response = await request(app).get('/api/version');
expect(response.status).toBe(200);
expect(response.body).toEqual({ version: '1.0.0' });

});

});
```
```
```

By adopting a thorough testing strategy using the appropriate tools and practices, development teams can catch bugs early, foster confidence in their code, and streamline the deployment process. Both unit and integration testing serve as critical components in maintaining the quality of DevOps initiatives, ultimately leading to smoother workflows and more reliable software.

Debugging and Performance Optimization Techniques

In the modern landscape of software development, robust applications are no longer limited to just functionality; they also require efficiency and ease of maintenance. Debugging and performance optimization are critical skills for developers working with TypeScript, a language that proudly combines the strengths of JavaScript with static typing. This chapter explores effective debugging strategies, tools, and techniques to enhance performance in TypeScript applications.

1. Introduction to Debugging in TypeScript

Debugging is the process of identifying and resolving bugs or issues in software code. The ability to perform effective debugging is crucial in delivering high-quality software. TypeScript's static typing and rich tooling enable developers to catch errors early in the development phase, thereby reducing the likelihood of runtime errors.

1.1 Benefits of TypeScript for Debugging

Static Typing: TypeScript's type system helps catch errors at compile time, reducing the amount of debugging needed during runtime.

Intellisense Support: Modern IDEs like Visual Studio Code provide excellent autocomplete and type inference features, which facilitate easier navigation and fewer coding mistakes.

Better Error Messages: TypeScript offers clearer and more informative error messages compared to plain JavaScript, aiding developers in troubleshooting issues more effectively.

2. Common Debugging Techniques ### 2.1 Console Logging

While it may seem rudimentary, using `console.log()` statements is still one of the simplest debugging techniques. TypeScript supports both `console.log()` and more structured logging mechanisms, enabling you to output variable states and flow control information.

```typescript
const sum = (a: number, b: number): number => {
console.log(`Adding ${a} and ${b}`);

return a + b;

}
```

```
` ` `
```

2.2 Using Breakpoints

Most modern IDEs offer debugging tools that allow you to set breakpoints in your code. TypeScript code can be executed in a debugging session, allowing you to pause execution and inspect variables, call stacks, and more.

Set Breakpoints: Click in the gutter next to the line number to set a breakpoint.

Step Through Code: Use "Step Over" and "Step Into" to navigate through your code.

Watch Expressions: Monitor the values of variables over time, aiding in understanding how data changes through execution.

2.3 Type Assertions and Type Guards

In situations where TypeScript's type inference may not suffice, utilizing type assertions or type guards can refine debugging efforts.

```typescript
function handleInput(input: unknown): string { if (typeof input === 'string') {

return input.toUpperCase();

}

throw new Error('Invalid input type');

}
```

2.4 Linting Tools

Integrating linting tools such as ESLint can drastically reduce errors by enforcing coding standards and checking for common programming mistakes during development. TypeScript has specific ESLint rules that ensure type safety and code quality.

3. Performance Optimization Techniques

Once you have successfully debugged your application, the next step is to ensure it performs optimally. Below are several techniques specifically tailored for optimizing TypeScript applications.

3.1 Analyzing Performance #### 3.1.1 Browser DevTools

Navigating through the built-in performance analysis tools offered by web browsers (like Chrome's DevTools or Firefox's performance tab) provides insights into bottlenecks and slowdowns in your application. These tools help profile CPU usage, memory consumption, and identify long task activities.

3.2 Minimizing Render Blocking

In single-page applications, reducing render-blocking resources can enhance performance. Techniques include:

- **Code Splitting**: Utilizing dynamic imports to load modules only when needed can significantly reduce the initial load time of the application.

```typescript
import('module-name').then(module => {
```

```
// Use module
});
```
```

**Lazy Loading Components**: For front-end frameworks like Angular or React, components can be lazy- loaded to defer loading until required.

### 3.3 Optimizing Data Structures

Choose efficient data structures that suit your use case. TypeScript allows you to define interfaces and types that lend themselves to improved performance. Here are some strategies:

**Use Maps for Keyed Collections**: Where appropriate, using `Map` over plain objects can yield better performance due to optimized key searches.

**Immutable Data**: Using immutable data structures, when applicable, can reduce the need for copying collections and enhance performance through optimizations in change detection (especially in frameworks like React).

### 3.4 Leveraging Async Patterns

Implement asynchronous programming patterns effectively to prevent blocking the main thread, which helps maintain a responsive user interface. Use `async/await` effectively to manage asynchronous code flows.

```typescript
async function fetchData(url: string): Promise<Response>
{ const response = await fetch(url);
```
```

```
return response.json();

}

` ` `
```

3.5 Tree Shaking and Minification

Utilize build tools—like Webpack and Rollup—that support tree shaking and minification to drop unused code and reduce bundle sizes. TypeScript's `tsconfig.json` can be configured to support ES modules, enabling tree shaking capabilities.

3.6 Caching Strategies

Implement caching mechanisms using local storage, session storage, or indexedDB to store data that does not change frequently. This practice can drastically reduce the need for repeated network requests, enhancing application performance.

By effectively employing TypeScript's powerful features, leveraging modern debugging tools, and implementing robust optimization strategies, you can create applications that are not only functional but also performant and maintainable.

Conclusion

In today's fast-paced technology landscape, the ability to automate, scale, and secure infrastructure is more critical than ever. As we've explored throughout this ebook, TypeScript emerges as a powerful ally for DevOps professionals seeking to enhance their workflows and increase efficiency. By leveraging TypeScript's strong typing, modern syntax, and comprehensive tooling, you can streamline your infrastructure management while also improving the maintainability of your code.

As you've learned, TypeScript not only enhances collaboration among team members but also reduces the likelihood of bugs and runtime errors through its static typing features. This leads to cleaner, more reliable applications and scripts that are easier to debug and scale, which is crucial in a DevOps environment where speed and agility are paramount.

Throughout this journey, we've discussed various strategies for integrating TypeScript into your DevOps practices, from automated deployment pipelines to configuration management. We've also touched on how TypeScript can enhance your security posture by enabling better code quality and adherence to best practices, ensuring robust infrastructure that is resistant to vulnerabilities.

In conclusion, adopting TypeScript in your DevOps toolkit can unlock new levels of productivity and innovation. As you move forward, embrace the principles and techniques outlined in this book, and consider them not just as methods, but as a mindset that prioritizes automation, security, and scalability.

Remember, the world of DevOps is continuously evolving, and staying ahead of the curve will require ongoing learning and adaptation. Utilize the resources, tools, and knowledge you've gained here to continuously refine your approaches, enabling you and your team to harness the true potential of your infrastructure.

Thank you for embarking on this journey into the world of TypeScript for DevOps. May it serve as your secret weapon in conquering the challenges of modern infrastructure management, empowering you to deliver greater value with every deployment. Happy coding!

Biography

Adrian is a passionate innovator and a visionary in the world of **Miller**, blending deep expertise with a relentless drive to push boundaries. With a background rooted in **web development, TypeScript programming, and blockchain technology**, Adrian thrives at the intersection of cutting-edge technology and practical applications. His work in **web applications** has empowered countless developers and entrepreneurs to build scalable, high-performance digital solutions.

Beyond his technical prowess, Adrian is fueled by a love for problem-solving and creative innovation. Whether he's architecting blockchain solutions or refining his latest **TypeScript-powered application**, his mission is always the same—to simplify the complex and unlock new possibilities for others.

When he's not coding or writing, you'll find Adrian exploring the ever-evolving landscape of decentralized technology, mentoring aspiring developers, or experimenting with the latest web frameworks. His dedication to learning and sharing knowledge makes his work not just insightful but transformative.

Through this eBook, Adrian brings his expertise, passion, and real-world experience to guide readers on their own journey—offering not just knowledge, but a roadmap to success.

Glossary: TypeScript for DevOps

A

Agile

A methodology that emphasizes iterative development, collaboration, and flexibility. It encourages adaptive planning and rapid responses to change, which aligns well with the continuous integration and continuous deployment (CI/CD) practices in DevOps.

API (Application Programming Interface)

A set of protocols and tools for building software applications. In TypeScript, APIs can be defined with strict types, enhancing code clarity and reducing runtime errors.

B

Build Automation

A process that automates the creation of executable applications from source code. TypeScript can be integrated into build tools like Webpack or Gulp to streamline the development workflow.

Continuous Build

An automated procedure that builds a software project every time the source code changes, facilitating immediate testing and feedback. In TypeScript, this ensures that type checks and compilation errors are caught early.

C

CI/CD (Continuous Integration/Continuous Deployment)

A set of practices that automate the integration of code changes and the deployment of applications. Tools like Jenkins or GitHub Actions can be used to automate CI/CD pipelines for TypeScript applications.

Compiled Language

TypeScript is a superset of JavaScript that is compiled to JavaScript. This means TypeScript code is transformed into plain JavaScript, making it runnable in any JavaScript environment.

Containerization

The practice of packaging applications and their dependencies into isolated environments called containers. Tools like Docker are commonly used to containerize TypeScript applications, ensuring consistency across development, testing, and production environments.

D

DevOps

A set of practices that combine software development (Dev) and IT operations (Ops) aimed at shortening the development life cycle and delivering high-quality software. TypeScript plays a significant role in building reliable and maintainable code.

Deployment Pipeline

A series of steps that automate the process of deploying an application from development to production. TypeScript applications can be integrated into pipeline tools like

Azure DevOps or GitLab CI to facilitate smoother deployments.

E

Environment Configuration

The practice of setting up different environments (development, testing, production) with specific configurations. In TypeScript applications, `.env` files and configuration management can help manage environment-specific settings.

ESLint

A tool for identifying and fixing problems in JavaScript or TypeScript code. ESLint can enforce coding standards and help maintain code quality across a TypeScript codebase.

F

Frontend

The client-side part of an application that users interact with. TypeScript is frequently used in frontend development frameworks like Angular, React, or Vue.js, enhancing the robustness of client-side code.

G

Git

A version control system that tracks changes in source code during software development. TypeScript developers use Git to manage and collaborate on code changes.

GitHub Actions

A CI/CD service within GitHub that allows users to

automate their build, test, and deployment pipelines directly from their repositories. TypeScript projects can leverage GitHub Actions for continuous integration.

H

Hook

A method that allows users to "hook into" certain operations or events in the lifecycle of a component. In React applications using TypeScript, hooks enhance the development experience by making it easier to manage state and side effects.

I

Infrastructure as Code (IaC)

A practice of managing and provisioning computing infrastructure through code instead of manual processes. Tools like Terraform can be used to automate the deployment of the infrastructure that supports TypeScript applications.

J

Jest

A JavaScript testing framework that is widely used for testing TypeScript applications. Jest provides a simple and intuitive API to define tests and can run them in parallel, significantly speeding up the testing process.

L

Linter

A static code analysis tool that checks code for stylistic errors and programming bugs. TypeScript supports various linters (like ESLint) to ensure code quality and adherence to coding standards.

M

Microservices

An architectural style that structures an application as a collection of loosely coupled services. TypeScript can be used to develop microservices that communicate through APIs, enhancing scalability and maintainability.

N

Node.js

A runtime environment that allows the execution of JavaScript and TypeScript code on the server side. Many TypeScript applications are built on top of Node.js, leveraging its event-driven architecture.

P

Package Manager

A tool that automates the installation, upgrading, configuring, and removal of software packages. npm (Node Package Manager) and yarn are popular package managers used in TypeScript projects to manage dependencies.

R

Repository

A storage location for software packages, source code, or configurations. Version control systems like Git are used to manage repositories for TypeScript projects, facilitating collaboration and version management.

S

Scrum

An Agile framework for managing complex projects. Teams often use Scrum in conjunction with DevOps practices to deliver software iteratively and incrementally.

Static Typing

A feature of TypeScript that allows developers to define variable types at compile time, reducing runtime errors and making the codebase more predictable and maintainable.

T

TypeScript

A superset of JavaScript that adds optional static typing, interfaces, and other features. TypeScript enables developers to write more reliable and maintainable code, making it a favored choice in the DevOps community.

Type Definitions

Files that provide type information about libraries and frameworks in TypeScript. These files help TypeScript understand the types used in third-party JavaScript libraries, enhancing the development experience.

U

Unit Testing

A software testing method where individual components of an application are tested in isolation. TypeScript supports unit testing with frameworks like Jest and Mocha, ensuring code reliability before deployment.

V

Version Control

A system that records changes to files or sets of files over time so that you can recall specific versions later. Git is the most prevalent version control system used with TypeScript projects in the DevOps context.

W

Workflow Automation

The practice of automating repetitive tasks in the software development process. In TypeScript development, various tools can automate tasks like code linting, testing, and deployment.

Webpack

A static module bundler for modern JavaScript applications. Especially in TypeScript projects, Webpack helps manage and optimize resources for production deployment.

www.ingramcontent.com/pod-product-compliance
Lightning Source LLC
LaVergne TN
LVHW052058060326
832903LV00061B/3379